T&T CLARK STUDY GUIDES TO THE OLD TESTAMENT

Ezra-Nehemiah

Series Editor

Adrian Curtis, University of Manchester, UK

Published in Association with the Society for
Old Testament Study

OTHER TITLES IN THE SERIES INCLUDE:

T&T CLARK STUDY GUIDES TO THE NEW TESTAMENT:

Ezra-Nehemiah: An Introduction and Study Guide

Israel's Quest for Identity

By Lena-Sofia Tiemeyer

Bloomsbury T&T Clark
An imprint of Bloomsbury Publishing Plc

B L O O M S B U R Y
LONDON · OXFORD · NEW YORK · NEW DELHI · SYDNEY

Bloomsbury T&T Clark

An imprint of Bloomsbury Publishing Plc

Imprint previously known as T&T Clark

50 Bedford Square	1385 Broadway
London	New York
WC1B 3DP	NY 10018
UK	USA

www.bloomsbury.com

BLOOMSBURY, T&T CLARK and the Diana logo are trademarks of Bloomsbury Publishing Plc

First published 2017

© Lena-Sofia Tiemeyer, 2017

Lena-Sofia Tiemeyer has asserted her right under the Copyright, Designs and Patents Act, 1988, to be identified as Author of this work.

British Library Cataloguing-in-Publication Data
A catalogue record for this book is available from the British Library.

ISBN: PB: 978-0-5676-7499-9
ePDF: 978-0-5676-7500-2
ePub: 978-0-5676-7501-9

Library of Congress Cataloging-in-Publication Data
A catalog record for this book is available from the Library of Congress.

Series: T&T Clark Study Guides to the Old Testament, volume 26

Cover design by clareturner.co.uk

Typeset by Deanta Global Publishing Services, Chennai, India

Contents

2   The Composition History of Ezra-Nehemiah   39

3   The Situation in Post-Monarchic Yehud   67

4   The Marriage Crisis   85

List of Abbreviations

AOAT	Alter Orient und Altes Testament
BZAW	Beihefte zur Zeitschrift für die alttestamentliche Wissenschaft
FAT	Forschungen zum Alten Testament
HBM	Hebrew Bible Monographs
HTR	*Harvard Theological Review*
JAJS	Journal of Ancient Judaism Supplements
JBL	*Journal of Biblical Literature*
JHS	*Journal of Hebrew Scripture*
JJS	*Journal of Jewish Studies*
JQR	*Jewish Quarterly Review*
JSJ	*Journal for the Study of Judaism*
JSJS	Supplements to the Journal for the Study of Judaism
JSOT	*Journal for the Study of the Old Testament*
JSOTS	Supplements to Journal for the Study of the Old Testament
JTS	*Journal of Theological Studies*
LHBOTS	Library of Hebrew Bible/Old Testament Studies
LSTS	Library of Second Temple Studies
NICOT	New International Commentary of the Old Testament
OBO	Orbis Biblicus et Orientalis
OTL	Old Testament Library
OTM	Oxford Theological Monographs
OtS	Oudtestamentische Studiën
SBL	Society of Biblical Literature
SBLDS	Society of Biblical Literature Dissertation Series
SBLMS	Society of Biblical Literature Monograph Series
SJLA	Studies in Judaism in Late Antiquity

STDJ	Studies on the Texts of the Desert of Judah
VT	*Vetus Testamentum*
VTS	Vetus Testamentum Supplements
WBC	Word Biblical Commentary
WMANT	Wissenschaftliche Monographien zum Alten und Neuen Testament
ZAW	*Zeitschrift für die alttestamentliche Wissenschaft*

Introduction

The books of Ezra and Nehemiah tell the story of the people in Yehud in the sixth and the fifth century BCE. This was a time of political and economic hardship. The people living in and around Jerusalem were eking out a living in a land that had been devastated by war. Some of the inhabitants had lived there since birth; others had come from Babylon where they, their parents, and grandparents had lived since the fall of Jerusalem in 586 BCE. Not only did they have to come to terms with poverty, they also had to negotiate different factions in the community who held divergent ideas on how the much-needed restoration should be carried out. While some may have argued that it would make economic sense to rebuild Jerusalem's city wall in order to generate income in the form of tax from traders, others may have maintained that such a building project would be (mis-)understood by the Persian overlords as an aggressive attempt to fortify the city. Furthermore, discussions may have become heated as to whether traders should be allowed to sell their goods every day of the week or whether the markets should be closed on the Sabbath in order to keep God's commandment.

This period was also a time of soul-searching and a quest for identity. Having lost their political autonomy and thus their national identity when the Neo-Babylonians sacked Jerusalem in 586 BCE, the people in Yehud had to find new ways of understanding and shaping their identity as distinct from that of the surrounding peoples. Most importantly, what made a person a Jew: their ethnicity, or their religious practices, or yet something even more elusive? Besides, once obtained, how could this fragile identity be preserved against threats from both within and without the community? In short, who was part of the community and who was not, and who was eligible to decide such matters? Again, the people of Yehud did not agree on the way forward. While some people may have desired a narrow definition of what it meant to be a Jew, others may have advocated a less stringent way of defining a person's identity.

The books of Ezra and Nehemiah provide glimpses of the issues that were current in the sixth and the fifth centuries BCE, by way of a curious assortment of first-person and third-person narratives, lists, letters and other types of records. Some of these texts may be genuine artefacts from these time periods, while others may constitute later reflections of this era. Together, they present the situation in Yehud in a motley fashion. The readers encounter different voices and different opinions and they often struggle to navigate the divergent opinions that are presented. The present Guide provides an overview of the various texts and the topics, concerns and disputes that they reflect, and it also zooms in on select key issues pertaining to the development of the text, its historical background(s), the quest for identity and its afterlife in Jewish and Christian traditions.

1

The Structure of Ezra-Nehemiah

In Jewish tradition, the books of Ezra and Nehemiah are preserved in a single scroll. This tradition has given rise to the notion that the two books, although they clearly were written by different authors and contain various types of written documents, form a single whole. Expressed differently, at one point in history, someone decided that it would be useful to read Ezra and Nehemiah as one literary unit. In parallel, the fact remains that they appear as two separate books in all printed bibles.

This issue – one scroll *versus* two books – is connected with not only the structure of the biblical text but also its history of composition. On the one hand, there is continuity in terms of dramatis personae throughout the two books, in that the character of Ezra appears not only in Ezra 7–10 but also in Nehemiah 8. Moreover, several themes recur in both books, most notably Ezra's and Nehemiah's objections to the marriages into which some men in their community had entered. At the same time, there are distinct differences in style between the two books, which warrant the view that we are dealing with two distinct books.

There is no easy way of untangling this issue. In ch. 1, we shall explore the issue of structure, while ch. 2 will be devoted to the issue of the gradual formation of Ezra-Nehemiah. As for now, I will follow the Jewish convention of referring to the books of Ezra and Nehemiah in the singular as Ezra-Nehemiah.

Ezra-Nehemiah is notorious for its structure – or the lack thereof. In order to understand many of the theories pertaining to the gradual development of Ezra-Nehemiah, it is imperative to have a clear view of the various types of material that are found in the scroll, as well as where the different sections begin and end.

Many studies deal with the overall structure of Ezra-Nehemiah in its present form. These studies do not take the prehistory of the text into account, but instead propose ways of making sense of the text as it is presented before the readers. The text is divided into three main sections: Ezra 1–6; Ezra 7–10; and Neh. 1–13. There is little disagreement regarding the individual and distinctive character of the two first sections (e.g. Japhet 1994: 190). In contrast, scholars disagree about the character and coherence of the third main section in Neh. 1–13. Is it one single section or does it rather consist of two, relatively independent parts? A few scholars maintain that Neh. 1–13 is structured in the same way as the preceding two sections and thus should be treated as one extended section. Talmon, for example, points out that Ezra 1–6, Ezra 7–10 and Neh. 1–13 all contain the same types of texts: Aramaic documents (Ezra 1–6 and Ezra 7–10), letters (Ezra 1–6 and Neh. 1–13), lists (all three sections), major festivals in Jerusalem (all three sections) and prayers (Ezra 7–10 and Neh. 1–13) (Talmon 1987: 358–9). It is more common, however, to differentiate between Neh. 1–6(7) on the one hand, and Neh. (7)8–13 on the other. Childs, for instance, argues that Ezra-Nehemiah has a four-part structure which focuses on four key events: the reconstruction of the temple (Ezra 1–6); Ezra's marriage reform (Ezra 7–10); Nehemiah's rebuilding of the city walls (Neh. 1–6); and the reconstruction of the community in Yehud (Neh. 7–13) (Childs 1979: 632–63).

It is also important to recognize that a few scholars read the entire Ezra-Nehemiah as one coherent narrative, the structure of which reaches across the boundaries of Ezra and Nehemiah. Notably, Eskenazi postulates a thematic, three-part structure: Ezra 1.1-4 (decree to the community to build the temple); Ezra 1.5–Neh. 7.72 (the community builds the temple); and

Neh. 8.1–13.31 (the community celebrates the completion of the temple according to the Torah) (Eskenazi 1988: 175–6).

In the following pages, we shall proceed carefully through the material of Ezra-Nehemiah. I shall try to establish the delimitations of the various subsections, offer a survey of the content of a given subsection (*synopsis*) and highlight matters that warrant further attention (*issues*).

Ezra 1–6

Ezra 1–6 constitutes the first main building block of Ezra-Nehemiah. These six chapters do not form a homogenous whole, however, but contain several smaller building blocks such as letters and lists that do not, at least at a first glance, seem to belong together. At the same time, several unifying factors make it reasonable to treat Ezra 1–6 as a textual (but not an authorial) unit. The main message of Ezra 1–6 can be captured by its two main dramatis personae: Joshua and Zerubbabel, who together are presented as the restorers of the city of Jerusalem.

Ezra 1.1-4

Synopsis

Ezra 1.1-4 contains a proclamation by Cyrus, the Persian emperor, 'in the first year of King Cyrus'. This dating formula is ambivalent for historical reasons: Cyrus became king over Persia in 559/8 BCE and over Babylon in 539 BCE. Ezra 1.1 presumably refers to the latter date. In his proclamation, Cyrus states that YHWH has commissioned him to build him a house in Jerusalem. (God will be referred to as YHWH throughout the Guide.) Cyrus also proclaims that any person belonging to YHWH's people may travel to Jerusalem.

Issues

Ezra 1.1-3a overlaps with the last two verses in 2 Chronicles (36.22-23). This overlap influences our understanding of the origins of the various texts in Ezra-Nehemiah, as well as of the identity of the person (the editor) who created the final form of Ezra-Nehemiah or at least of Ezra 1–6. Is the editor of Ezra-Nehemiah identical with the Chronicler responsible for putting together 1–2 Chronicles (ch. 2: NB cross-references of this type refer to chapters in the Guide)?

Ezra 1.1-4 is written in Hebrew. This fact makes it relatively clear that we are not reading the original proclamation, as neither Cyrus nor his secretaries are likely to have been fluent in this language; they would rather have used Aramaic, the lingua franca of the Persian Empire. Does Ezra 1.1-4 therefore record a *translation* of an authentic edict, or is it a *fictional creation* (ch. 2)?

Ezra 1.5-11

Synopsis

Ezra 1.5-11 contains the response of the Babylonian diaspora community, that is, the community of exiles whose ancestors had been forced to migrate to Babylon before and after the destruction of Jerusalem in 586 BCE (v. 11). They decide to leave for Jerusalem and to bring with them their sacred treasures which the Babylonian king, Nebuchadnezzar, had taken as spoils at the time of the destruction of Jerusalem.

Issues

The treasures were given for safe keeping to 'Sheshbazzar, the prince of Judah'. The identity and historicity of this man is a key question in research. Did he exist and what was his role in the rebuilding of the temple? Alternatively, is he a fictional character and, if so, what function does he play in the narrative (ch. 5)?

Ezra 2.1-67

Synopsis

The next section in Ezra 2.1-67 does not contain a list of immigrants, as one would expect from the preceding Ezra 1.11, but a list of people who have left exile in Babylon and returned to their ancestral land in Judah or 'Yehud' as the province is called during the Persian period.

Issues

This list exists in a very similar form in Neh. 7.6-69. There is little doubt that we are dealing with the same list. This 'double' provides important insight into the origin of the various texts in Ezra-Nehemiah, as well as shedding light upon the work of its editors. First, which place – Ezra 2 or Nehemiah 7 – is the original place? Second, what functions does the list play in its two different literary locations (ch. 2)?

This list further raises historical issues. Who were these people, when did they arrive in Yehud and who were their leaders? Sheshbazzar who appeared in Ezra 1 is not mentioned here. Instead, the readers encounter new leaders in Ezra 2.2. Of these men, two names stand out: Zerubbabel and Joshua. These two figures are known from texts outside Ezra-Nehemiah, namely, in the prophetic texts of Haggai and Zechariah 1–6 (ch. 5). Finally, who is the third man, Nehemiah, who is listed in this verse? It is chronologically impossible for him to be the same man as the one who features in Neh. 1–13. Notably, the parallel verse in Neh. 7.7 lists Azariah as the fourth man, a name which brings the character of Ezra to mind (see further Blenkinsopp 1988: 85). Is this a curious coincidence or something more?

Ezra 2.68-70; 3.1-6, 7-13; 4.1-5

Synopsis

Ezra 2.68-70, the first part of this section, resembles Neh. 7.70-73. It is not a list, though, but a narrative which tells how the exiles arrived in Jerusalem. Verse 68 can be read as the direct continuation of Ezra 1.11, that is, the text prior to the list.

Ezra 3.1-6 appears to continue the narrative that was begun in Ezra 2.68-70. It tells how in the seventh month, the two leaders Joshua and Zerubbabel began building the altar and offered sacrifices (v. 2). At that time, however, the foundation of the temple had not yet been laid (v. 6). Ezra 3.7-13 provides more information about the building work on the temple.

Ezra 4.1-5 introduces new characters, namely, the 'adversaries of Judah and Benjamin'. They are identified as the foreigners who were settled in the northern kingdom of Israel in the eighth century BCE, and who by now have become assimilated and adopted the Israelite cult. Their offer to participate in the rebuilding of the temple is rejected, which creates a situation of hostility which, in turn, causes a delay in the building work.

Issues

There are two interrelated structural decisions that the readers have to make at this point. First, is Ezra 2.68 the continuation of Ezra 1.11 or of Ezra 2.67? Second, does Ezra 3.1 begin a new narrative or does it follow on immediately after 2.68-

70? These two questions impact our estimation of the depicted *chronology* of these texts. Ezra 1 describes matters shortly after 539 BCE, as noted by Ezra 1.1. If we read Ezra 2.68–3.6 as the direct continuation of Ezra 1, the 'seventh month' in Ezra 3.1 must also be in 539 BCE during the reign of the Persian emperor, Cyrus. This scenario is, however, problematized by the appearance of Joshua and Zerubbabel in Ezra 3.2, who according to Haggai and Zechariah 1–6 are associated with the year 520 BCE and the reign of Darius I (ch. 5).

These questions also influence our understanding of the *literary structure* of the text. Whereas the protagonist in Ezra 1 is Sheshbazzar, the protagonists in Ezra 3.1–4.5 are Joshua and Zerubbabel. The latter two men are already known to us from the list in Ezra 2. From a literary perspective, Ezra 2.68-70 thus appears to belong with Ezra 1, while Ezra 3.1–4.5 appears to belong with Ezra 2. At the same time, all of Ezra 2.68–4.5 appears to provide a continuous narrative. When read together, the readers are given the impression that Sheshbazzar, Zerubbabel and Joshua are contemporary with one another and that they were all active during the reign of Cyrus. This impression is further strengthened by the reference to Cyrus in Ezra 4.3-4. Moreover, since only Sheshbazzar appears with his title ('the prince'), the readers of the continuous text receive the impression that he is the main leader (Japhet 1982).

The notion of the 'adversaries of Judah and Benjamin' also raises some questions. In particular, who were they and what was their relationship to the returning exiles? Their identification with the people of Samaria is not without problems. For example, are the 'adversaries of Judah and Benjamin' to be understood as the leaders of the province of Samaria, or rather as (some) people who remained in the land during the exile (ch. 3)?

Ezra 4.6-24

Synopsis

Up until Ezra 4.5, the readers have been given the impression that they are reading about the last half of the sixth century and about events that were taking place during the reign of Cyrus. Ezra 4.6 challenges this impression as it catapults the readers about fifty years forward into the fifth century BCE. We learn in v. 6 that 'they' lodged a written complaint in the reign of the Persian monarch, Ahasuerus (Xerxes 486–665 BCE). The identity of the plaintiff should logically be the aforementioned 'adversaries' that the readers encountered in the preceding vv. 1-5. Verse 7 then mentions what is presumably another letter, this time written to the Persian king, Artaxerxes

(I) (465–423 BCE). Verses 8-11aα feature further introductions to these letters. What follows are a sequence of letters written in Aramaic (vv. 11aβ-16, 17-22), as well as a short narrative about the repercussions of these letters in Yehud: the work on the temple came to a halt until the second year of the reign of Darius (I) (Ezra 4.24).

Issues

The set of introductions in vv. 8-11 begins an extended part of Ezra that is written in Aramaic (Ezra 4.8–6.18). This language lends an air of authenticity to the royal correspondence which, as mentioned before, would have been composed in Aramaic, that is, the official language of correspondence of the Persian Empire. As in the case of Ezra 1.1-4, the question nevertheless arises as to whether these letters are transcripts of authentic historical records or fictional accounts (ch. 3).

The reference to the 'reign of Darius' in Ezra 4.24 is deeply problematic from a chronological perspective. If this reference indicates Darius I, which is very likely, then the current text of Ezra is giving the (historically incorrect) impression that Darius I reigned *after* Xerxes and Artaxerxes. The alternative is to look at this issue from a literary perspective. Ezra 4.24 clearly refers back to the reference to Darius in Ezra 4.5. It is thus possible to relate to Ezra 4.24 as a 'repetitive resumption', that is, a literary tool which effectively places a parenthesis around the in-between-lying documents (Blenkinsopp 1988: 111).

Ezra 5.1-2, 3-5, 6-17

Synopsis

The short section of Ezra 5.1-2 connects the narrative(s) in Ezra 1–6 with the prophetic material in Haggai and Zechariah 1–6. It further serves to emphasize that the temple building project is fully sanctified by YHWH and supported by the words of his prophets. More indirectly, it dates the material to the reign of Darius I. The narrative continues in Ezra 5.3-5. The chronological reference that is hinted at in vv. 1-2 is confirmed by v. 5 with an explicit reference to Darius. The subsequent Ezra 5.6-17 features yet another royal correspondence, this time between Tattenai, governor of the satrapy (the technical term for a large region in the Persian Empire) often called Beyond the River (the westernmost province/satrapy in the Persian Empire), and the Persian monarch Darius, seeking again to impede the building project.

Issues

This passage, as well as the later passage in Ezra 7.1-10, emphasizes the benevolence of the Persian ruler. This is a clear literary strategy which sets Ezra-Nehemiah apart from many other biblical books, where foreign kings are described as acting cruelly and destructively towards Israel. In Ezra, the foreign ruler is still God's tool, but he is now working for Israel's benefit (ch. 3).

Ezra 6.1-12, 13-18

Synopsis

Darius I's response appears in Ezra 6.1-12, which alludes to Cyrus's proclamation in Ezra 1.1-4. After a search in the archives in the Persian city of Ecbatana (vv. 1-2), a scroll was found which confirms the right of the returned exiles to rebuild the temple in Jerusalem. Darius I's response to Tattenai, 'the governor of Beyond the River' includes a quote of its content (vv. 3-5) and further instructions to allow the Jews to continue with the temple rebuilding project (vv. 6-12). This letter leads Tattenai to call out the royal instructions and the Jews are able, with additional support from the prophecies by Haggai and Zechariah, to finish the building project and to dedicate the new temple (vv. 13-18).

Issues

The material in Ezra 6.6-18 stands out in the sense that it uses the term 'Jew'. So far, the other documents have referred to the people building the temple as 'returning exiles'. It is in line with the royal decree genre not to differentiate between the various groups of people in Yehud at the time, but instead simply to refer to all of them as 'Jews'. The reference to 'Tattenai' raises several questions. Who was Tattenai and what was his authority in Yehud (ch. 3)?

Ezra 6.19-22

Synopsis

Ezra 6.19-22 jumps forward in time to the fourteenth day of the first month. It tells how the exiles and 'those people who had joined them' celebrated the

Passover together. At this point, the narrative returns to Hebrew again, and the terminology reverts to 'exiles' rather than 'Jews'.

Issues

These verses have been noted by scholars for two key reasons. First, they provide information about the Jewish calendar. The celebration in Ezra 6.19-22 follows the date established by Exod. 12.1-6; Lev. 23.5-6; Num. 9.3, 5 and so on. This may show that these texts were known at this time. In parallel, this passage reveals that the New Year (i.e. the first month) must have taken place in spring rather than, as in the current Jewish calendar, in the autumn (on the first day of *Tishri*).

Second, these verses are important insofar as they allude to a certain level of cooperation and harmony between the different parts of the society in Yehud. They also raise the question of the identity of the people who joined the exiles. Were they but other inhabitants of Yehud (henceforth 'Judahites') who had been left in the land in 586 BCE (ch. 4)?

Ezra 7–10

The final four chapters of the book of Ezra constitute the second main section of Ezra-Nehemiah. They are often called the 'Ezra Memoir' (EM) because Ezra is the first-person narrator. Much can be said in favour of treating these four chapters as a single, coherent textual unit with one key message: Ezra is the restorer of the Jewish community in Jerusalem.

Ezra 7.1-10

Synopsis

The narrative which begins in Ezra 7 changes the time frame of the narrative again. We are now firmly in the reign of Artaxerxes. We also meet a new character, Ezra. He is described as a diaspora Jew, living in Babylon where he was a 'scribe skilled in the Law of Moses'. In addition, he is given a priestly pedigree, going all the way back to Aaron. With the Persian king's blessing, Ezra sets out with a group of primarily clerical personnel and arrives in Jerusalem to study, observe and teach the law of YHWH.

Issues

The chronological references in this passage are ambiguous, insofar as there were several Artaxerxes. Most scholars claim that Ezra 7.1 refers to the reign of Artaxerxes I, which would place the narrative in the fifth century BCE. Alternatively, the text may refer to the reign of Artaxerxes II. In our evaluation of these options, we need to distinguish between history and literature. Beginning with the literary question, the readers of the book of Ezra are not being informed about multiple monarchs bearing the same name; rather their natural assumption would be that this Artaxerxes is the same as the author of the letter in Ezra 4. Looking at the issue historically, the question is whether the historical person named Ezra was active in Yehud in the fifth or in the fourth century BCE, that is, under the reign of Artaxerxes I or Artaxerxes II. This question, in turn, has consequences for the relative dating of the historical activity of the two protagonists Ezra and Nehemiah: did Ezra arrive and act in Yehud before or after Nehemiah? (Blenkinsopp 1988: 139–44, cf. ch. 3).

The description of Ezra as a 'scribe' raises questions concerning his level of authority. Just as a 'secretary' in English can range from the secretary of state to a typist, so too the term 'scribe' could describe a person with great authority as well as a person who was good at copying texts. The description of Ezra in 7.6 appears to suggest the former. The character of Ezra is depicted as a man with direct contact with and influence over the Persian monarch (ch. 3).

This description of Ezra provokes additional issues. Was Ezra a historical person or a literary figure or both? If literary, how well does the literary depiction of Ezra correspond with historical reality? Can we claim that Ezra was a powerful man who was authorized by the Persian Empire to carry out changes in Yehud, or are we rather dealing with a fictional narrative about a pious Jew who, like Daniel and Esther (and Nehemiah, see below), reached a high position in the diaspora (ch. 3)?

In the same way, what is the significance of Ezra's priestly lineage, not only historically but also as part of the plot progression of Ezra 7–10? From a literary perspective, his impeccable pedigree assures the readers that Ezra's understanding of the law is rooted in the pre-exilic traditions. It also serves to given him authority in matters of the temple (Eskenazi 1988: 136), even though no text in the Hebrew Bible describes him as the High Priest. Furthermore, the depiction of Ezra as a priest creates a neat parallel between the two ruling pairs in Ezra-Nehemiah. In the same way as Zerubbabel and Joshua present a diarchy between secular and cultic power (cf. Zech. 3–4), so

Nehemiah and Ezra represent the governor and the priest (Japhet 1982: 94, see further ch. 5).

Ezra 7.11, 12-26

Synopsis

Ezra 7.11 introduces the royal letter which follows in vv. 12-26. The letter is quoted in Aramaic, which lends it a touch of authenticity (cf. above). It assigns an astonishing degree of power and responsibility to Ezra: (1) to inquire about Yehud and Jerusalem with respect to the Law of his God; (2) to carry substantial amounts of silver and gold to the temple in Jerusalem, combined with the authority to do with these treasures as he sees fit; and (3) to appoint magistrates and judges who will judge the people in the Beyond the River satrapy and the jurisdiction to punish those who disobey.

Issues

Is this letter genuine, in the sense that the historical Persian monarch assigned this amount of power to a Babylonian Jew and this amount of riches to the Jerusalem temple? This depends to a large extent upon the aforementioned question of Ezra's status as a 'scribe'. It is possible to envision a historical scenario where the Persian king empowered a loyal representative of the local population with a high degree of power to carry out strategic changes in the administration of that population. It is equally possible that the letter is fictional and that it was purpose-written by the authors/editors of the book of Ezra to fit into the Ezra narrative (ch. 3).

On a literary level, the letter bolsters the readers' expectations concerning the character of Ezra, who has so far in the narrative not said a word. Who is this person with this enormous power? When Ezra appears later, the contrast is striking. It is possible that the readers will think: here is this person, clothed with all the power of the Persian Empire, yet he is unable to enforce a single divorce! It is, however, equally possible that the readers will consider Ezra an exemplary humble person who, despite all his power, chooses to plead with the people rather than to use brutal force (Eskenazi 1988: 137–8).

The letter uses the term 'Law of God'. What did its author (either the Persian monarch [if the letter is genuine] or the Jewish author [if the letter is fictional]) mean when employing this term? Did he refer to a set body of texts (such as the Torah/Pentateuch or a part thereof) that was available at the time of writing, or did he use this expression more loosely to describe an ideal law that may or may not have existed in written form? Further, did the term denote already existing and authoritative laws or did it rather represent the expectation that Ezra was to coin suitable laws and then to teach them? (See further Blenkinsopp 1988: 152–7, cf. ch. 3).

Ezra 7.27-28; 8.1-14

Synopsis

The language changes back to Hebrew again in Ezra 7.27. In addition, in v. 28 the narrative voice changes from the third person to the first person. The prayer and the subsequent declaration of resolve to go (to Jerusalem), expressed in vv. 27-28, is presumably voiced by Ezra himself. The prayer itself focuses on the temple in Jerusalem, that is, the second point on Ezra's to-do list, and on the Persian king's support of this endeavour. There is no mention of either the Law of God or the appointment of magistrates (Blenkinsopp 1988: 160). Ezra 8.1 introduces a list of people and their extended families who, together with Ezra, left Babylon for Jerusalem (vv. 2-14).

Issues

As the text stands, the list of names in vv. 2-14 is part of Ezra's first-person speech (8.1). Alternatively, the list in vv. 2-14 is a later insertion and the first-person speech in v. 1 is a redactional addition which serves to connect the prayer in Ezra 7.27-28 with the list (ch. 2).

Ezra 8.15-36

Synopsis

Ezra's first-person narrative continues/restarts in v. 15. Verses 15-30 provide a travel diary of Ezra and his companions, as they prepare for and set out from Babylon to Jerusalem, while vv. 31-36 depict how they safely reached their destination. Upon arrival, Ezra and his companions handed over the money and the temple vessels that they had carried, offered up sacrifices to YHWH and delivered the king's messages to the Persian officials in Yehud. It is fair to say that vv. 31-36 aim to record that the royal instructions were carried out to the letter.

Issues

The reference to the Persian officials raises both historical and literary issues. What were the power relations between Ezra on the one hand and these officials on the other? This question has both a historic and a literary dimension. Furthermore, how does the description of these officials in Yehud tally with the historical information that we have about Persian administration? (See further Grabbe 1998: 32; cf. ch. 3).

Ezra 9.1-5, 6-15

Synopsis

Ezra 9.1-2 tells how the leaders approached Ezra and informed him that a number of Judahite men had married women from the local population and thus committed a religious crime. Upon hearing this report, Ezra tore his clothes and his hair, then sat in a stupor while people sympathetic to his point of view gathered around him, and began to pray at the time of the evening sacrifice (vv. 3-5).

Issues

This account speaks of women from seven people groups (the Canaanites, Hittites, Perizzites, Jebusites, Ammonites, Moabites, Egyptians and Edomites). At the time of Ezra, some of these people no longer existed as distinct ethnic groups (e.g. the Jebusites). This statement is most likely a reference to and also an interpretation of select material in the Pentateuch (Gen. 15.19-20; Deut. 7.1-5; 23.4-8 [Eng. 3-7]). What has troubled several scholars is the exact identity of these women. Were they really 'foreigners' in the sense of speaking a different language and having a different culture, or were they rather fellow Judahites with the distinction, crucial from the perspective of the author of Ezra 9–10 (but not necessarily for themselves), that they had not been in exile but instead were the descendants of those who had stayed in the land after the fall of Jerusalem in 586 BCE? As we shall see further below, this so-called marriage crisis characterizes also the time of Nehemiah. These 'intermarriages' and the subsequent divorces of the 'foreign' women constitute a very important topic in research, not least because of the ethical and moral issues that these actions raise when they are being read today. All of ch. 4 will therefore be devoted to this issue.

Synopsis

The rest of Ezra 9 contains what may be labelled as either a prayer or a public confession. The text alternates between Ezra speaking in the first person singular and in the first person plural. In the prayer/confession, Ezra thanks God for his care and for the Persian king's benevolent attitude towards the returned exiles. He further urges those people listening to his speech not to allow their children to marry outside the community, lest the land itself will become ritually impure. He also takes responsibility for the sin of intermarriage. This prayer/confession is well integrated into its literary context and there are few reasons to treat it as secondary.

Issues

Some aspects of this prayer/confession cause consternation. In particular, v. 9 notably mentions of a protective wall around Jerusalem. According to the plot progression in Ezra-Nehemiah (cf. the chronological issues above), Nehemiah has not yet arrived in Yehud and thus the wall is still in ruins. Alternatively, reading the text of Ezra-Nehemiah in its present order, this statement may be understood metaphorically as a reference to the Persian support of the temple building project (referring back to the opposition in Ezra 4–6) (Blenkinsopp 1988: 184, cf. ch. 2).

Ezra 10.1-17, 18-44

Synopsis

In Ezra 10.1 until the end of the book, the narrative refers to Ezra in the third person. Ezra's prayer/confession caused 'a great assembly' to gather around Ezra. As their representative, Shecaniah, the son of Jehiel, declare: (1) they realize that the intermarriages are a sin; and (2) they are thus committed to expel all the foreign women from their midst, whereupon the gathered people take an oath to carry out this decision. Ezra continues to mourn the sins of the community and a proclamation was issued which commands all the returning exiles to gather in Jerusalem (v. 7).

Subsequently, 'all the men of Judah and Benjamin' gathered in Jerusalem in the ninth month, on the twentieth day of the month (v. 9). Ezra accuses the men of having acted faithlessly by marrying foreign women; the entire assembly agrees, yet also asks to be able to return to their own towns (as it is cold and rainy) and to have additional time to act upon Ezra's instructions. Ezra appoints local leaders to oversee the inquiry. By the first day of the tenth month, the matter was reported as being sorted out (v. 17, for a positive evaluation of Ezra's behaviour and leadership ability, see Eskenazi 1988: 140-1).

The concluding section (vv. 18-44) contains a long list of people who had married foreign women, including a number of priests, Levites and other temple personnel. Verse 44 concludes that all the listed men sent away their wives and children.

Issues

When reading only the book of Ezra, the narrative ends with the resolution that 'they had dealt with all the men who had married foreign women' (Ezra 10.17), a statement that is subsequently corroborated by the ensuing list. At the same time, this is a rather sad resolution (from the perspective of the women and the children involved, but potentially also from the readers' point of view) and there is a sense that the book demands a continuation. What happened to these women and children? What happened to the community in Yehud (Grabbe 1998: 38)?

Moreover, when reading all of Ezra-Nehemiah, this ending appears in a different light. From a literary perspective, the end of Ezra creates a problem when it is being read together with Neh. 13.23-31. In the latter section, Nehemiah observes a number of Jews who had married foreign women and makes them take an oath not to do so. The readers cannot help but wonder whether Ezra really dealt with the matter or whether he instead failed. Alternatively, did Ezra deal with the matter but it then recurred? Yet again, looking at the matter historically, is it possible that Nehemiah preceded Ezra, observed the matter, but that Ezra dealt with the issue later in a more permanent manner? (ch. 2)

Nehemiah 1–7

The third main building block of Ezra-Nehemiah contains the first six (or seven) chapters of the book of Nehemiah. Because they are presented as narrated by Nehemiah, they are often called the 'Nehemiah Memoirs' (NM). Although several passages disrupt the general flow of the textual block, the material can be read fruitfully as one continuous narrative, which is focused around one person and one matter: Nehemiah and his task to restore the city of Jerusalem.

Nehemiah 1.1-11

Synopsis

Nehemiah 1 opens with a brief headline which introduces the protagonist: Nehemiah, son of Hacaliah. He is present at the imperial court at Susa, the capital of the Persian Empire, where he is informed about the hardship of the Jewish community in Yehud and about the sorry state of the city wall of Jerusalem. After weeping and fasting for a few days, Nehemiah turns to God in prayer. He confesses the sins that he and his ancestors have committed and reminds God of his promise to gather the people together if they repent. Immediately after the prayer, Nehemiah states his profession: he was the king's cupbearer.

Issues

This passage is dated to the month of *Kislev* in the twentieth year (Neh. 1.1). Notably, the name of the king is not mentioned, leaving the reader a bit at a loss. If one reads Ezra-Nehemiah sequentially, however, the readers may assume that we are still in the reign of Artaxerxes (cf. Ezra 7.7), a mere thirteen years later.

Yet again, the readers who have just finished reading Ezra may be a bit surprised at both the news and Nehemiah's reaction to it. The impression given in Ezra 9–10 was not that of a destroyed city and a community in great distress. Furthermore, Nehemiah does not mention the intermarriages in his prayer. The readers thus begin to wonder what has happened in the interim of thirteen years (Grabbe 1998: 40).

The discrepancy between Ezra 10 and Nehemiah 1 in terms of the portrayal of the community and the city wall is one among several factors which has caused a number of scholars to question the relative chronology of Ezra's and Nehemiah's journeys to Jerusalem. Rather than accepting the chronology encouraged by a sequential reading of the material, namely, that Ezra preceded Nehemiah, they ask whether it would not make more sense to assume that Nehemiah arrived in Jerusalem prior to Ezra (ch. 3).

Nehemiah 2.1-10

Synopsis

Neh. 2.1 assures the readers that the narrative indeed took place during the reign of Artaxerxes. Nehemiah describes how while he is serving wine to the king, the king comments on Nehemiah's sad appearance, and how Nehemiah requests and is granted leave to go to Jerusalem in order to help in rebuilding the city. Nehemiah further manages to obtain letters addressed to key people in authority in Yehud to ensure that he will be given the necessary building material. Nehemiah arrives in Yehud, accompanied by an escort of captains and horsemen, with the royal letters to the governors of the Beyond the River satrapy. At this point, the readers encounter two hitherto unknown antagonists, namely, Sanballat the Horonite and Tobiah, the Ammonite 'servant' (v. 10).

Issues

The man Sanballat is one of the few characters in Ezra-Nehemiah who is known from extra-biblical sources. For example, letters from Elephantine (in Egypt) mention the name Sanballat (*COS* 3: 116, 130) and a bulla (a kind of seal: an inscribed piece of clay used as an authentication or security device) from Wadi ed-Dâliyeh (a group of caves near Jericho) names a Sanballat, who was governor of Samaria during the reign of Darius III (336–330 BCE) (*COS* 2: 204). There are, however, historical problems with this identification, most pertinently the fact Sanballat mentioned in the aforementioned papyri lived during the reign of Artaxerxes II, that is, around 408 BCE (see further Tiemeyer 2005: 877–80). An earlier text, found among the Lachish Ostraca (a series of letters written on clay shards, found in the Judean mountains), normally dated to the period before the fall of Jerusalem in 586 BCE, refers to a 'Tobiah, servant of the king' (Lachish 3, lines 19–21, *COS* 3: 78–90).

The historical background of the events described in Nehemiah's Memoirs (NM) is a much debated topic in scholarship. Exploring the historicity of the NM, scholars seek to fit the historical data known from extra-biblical material with the depiction of the events in Yehud in the NM. Nehemiah presents one perspective, namely, that of a returned diaspora Jew. There is, however, always another side, namely, the perspective of those Jews and non-Jews living in Yehud at the time of his arrival who for political, economic and/or religious reasons did not approve of Nehemiah's programme of reform (cf. Rom-Shiloni 2013: 33–47).

Another issue is Persia's involvement in and encouragement of the building of the city wall. Why would it be in the imperial interest to build a wall around Jerusalem? Walls have two main functions: to keep enemies out and to control the produce that is being brought in (for purpose of taxation). What would Persia gain from this (ch. 3)?

Nehemiah 2.11-20

Synopsis

Nehemiah arrives in Jerusalem and describes his first adventure there: a nightly walk around Jerusalem in order to estimate the damage to the city and to establish the order of priority in its restoration. He concludes that the rebuilding of the city wall is the most urgent matter. This decision is met with the disapproval of the aforementioned two antagonists Sanballat and Tobiah, as well as of a new character, Geshem, the Arab, yet Nehemiah declares his will to continue with his rebuilding plans under God's auspices.

Issues

Given the first-person narrative, NM is very one-sided and presents only Nehemiah's perspective. Experienced readers are aware that the narrative is biased, yet even they cannot access the counter-narrative but have to make do with reading between the lines. What is clear from the extant text is, though, that Nehemiah did not enjoy the support of the entire community; the question remains as to the size and influence of his support group.

Nehemiah 3.1-32

Synopsis

The narrative continues to report that the various groups of people involved in the wall building project set out to do their bit of the wall. This chapter lists the names of the people, headed by the High Priest Eliashib, and specifies which part of the wall they built. Nehemiah does not feature as the first-person narrator, but this in itself does not necessarily mean that this list is not part of Nehemiah's Memoir.

Issues

This passage raises a historical question, insofar as scholars have been trying to establish what it can tell us about the historical extent of Jerusalem in the fifth century BCE. Does it provide historical data and, if so, how does it compare with the available archaeological data (ch. 3)?

Further, what is the origin of this list? As always when dealing with Ezra-Nehemiah, we have to ask whether this list was composed to make a literary/ theological point in the narrative, or whether this list was an independent historical artefact (that existed in an archive somewhere) which the editors of Ezra-Nehemiah at one stage of the composition incorporated into their narrative. In both cases, the question remains as to what function it plays in the final text of Ezra-Nehemiah (ch. 2).

The fact that Eliashib heads this list is interesting due to Nehemiah's later negative view of the man (cf. Neh. 13.4-9, 28). This fact may, in turn, suggest that this list was not composed by Nehemiah (cf. Grabbe 1998: 43).

Nehemiah 4.1-6, 7-14, 15-23 [Heb. 3.33-38; 4.1-8, 9-17]

Synopsis

Nehemiah appears again in Neh. 4.1-6 [Heb. 3.33-38]. He describes anew Sanballat's and Geshem's antagonistic attitudes towards the wall building project and quotes their taunts. In response, Nehemiah turns to God and asks for his vengeance upon the opponents. Nehemiah further narrates how the people nevertheless were resolved to continue with the building project.

The saga continues in Neh. 4.7-14 [Heb. 4.1-8], where Nehemiah continues to face and also to battle the resistance raised by a few individuals (Sanballat, Tobiah) as well as a number of people groups (Arabs, Ammonites, Ashdodites). The latter began to plot against the builders and to spread threats, to which Nehemiah responds with prayers and military caution as he posts guards around the building sites. He also gives encouraging speeches to his followers, reminding them of God's power and their duty to fight on behalf of their families.

Nehemiah reports that the antagonists were disheartened by his resolve, and the workers decided to return to their work on the walls. Half of the group built the wall and the other half protected them. Nehemiah also designed a watch system, so that the people would know when to assemble to fight in times of need. They laboured so intensely, according to Nehemiah, that the men kept their clothes on at all times and kept their weapons by their sides.

Issues

Nehemiah's prayer in Neh. 4.4-5 [Heb. 3.36-37] raises moral issues as its tone and its expressed wishes disturb most modern persons' sensibilities. Nehemiah equates opposition to him with opposition to God, and his plea to God to remember his opponents' iniquities and to allow them to be given over as plunder leaves a bad taste in the mouth. At the same time, the prayer fits its present literary context, where it conveys Nehemiah's dedication to the project, his single-mindedness and his belief that his project is blessed by God, and therefore will progress according to plans. The readers receive a deep impression of Nehemiah as a leader and as a human being (both as a historical person and literary character). To cite Eskenazi, 'Nehemiah's confidence is both endearing and irritating, as bravado often is' (Eskenazi 1988: 145). From a different perspective, Grabbe states that 'one wonders whether Nehemiah was not being unduly thin-skinned about the matter' (Grabbe 1998: 44).

In addition, as mentioned above, we need to distinguish between: (1) what Nehemiah wants us to believe; and (2) what really happened. Was the plot real but did not come to fruition due to Nehemiah's caution, or was the plot a figment of Nehemiah's imagination? Also, who were Nehemiah's antagonists, what positions did they have, did they have a valid point, and did they enjoy the support of a significant part of the population of Yehud? The name Tobiah (which can be translated as 'Yhwh is good'), for example, suggests that Tobiah's parents stemmed from a Jewish family. Neh. 6.17-19 further tells us that he was well connected through marriage with other important families in Yehud. Moreover, his epithet 'the servant' suggests that he was a high level official (cf. 'a civil servant'), yet it is also possible to read it as 'the slave'. The ambiguity of the term may, in fact, be intended in Nehemiah's account (see further Grabbe 1998: 46).

Nehemiah 5.1-13

Synopsis

The topic of the narrative changes in Nehemiah 5. Nehemiah is made aware of instances of social imbalance in Yehud, where the rich in the community are using their economic power over those who are poor, to the point of forcing the latter to enter into debt-slavery. Nehemiah is enraged when he hears this, restrains himself, calls an assembly and admonishes the people to solve this economic crisis and to cease abusing the system and instead to annul the debts. He receives an immediate response where those involved promise to make amends.

Issues

This story breaks the narrative about the building of the city wall. The continuation in Neh. 5.14-19 is clearly from a later time. This raises the question of its rhetorical function in its present place. According to Eskenazi, the section, speaking of obstacles from within, serves to contrast the obstacles from without (i.e. from Sanballat etc.) in Neh. 3.33–4.17 (Eskenazi 1988: 78). The discerning readers may, however, ponder whether the threat from Sanballat and Tobiah may actually have constituted obstacles from within.

Nehemiah 5.14-19

Synopsis

In the next section (vv. 14-19), Nehemiah draws attention to a later time, namely, those twelve years when he served as governor in Yehud. During that time, Nehemiah and his fellow kinsmen rejected their food allowance and bought no land. Instead, Nehemiah prepared a meal for 150 people in order to help the (poor) people. In this manner, so we learn from Nehemiah, he differed from the previous governors who had acted out of self-interest and (only) sought to increase their own wealth. This example serves to emphasize the need to act generously and to prioritize the welfare of the community. It also seeks to shame the audience into following Nehemiah's example.

Issues

This passage contains the intriguing reference to 'the former governors' (see further Williamson 1988). Who were they? Some scholars argue that they must have been non-Jewish governors (e.g. Alt 1953), while others maintain that these previous governors were Jewish men (Avigad 1976).

Did Nehemiah include Zerubbabel in this list who, at least according to the book of Haggai, was the governor of Yehud in the latter part of the sixth century BCE?

To modern eyes, this passage portrays Nehemiah at his noblest. Who would not applaud his actions to relieve debt and to care for the undeservingly poor? As Grabbe highlights, however, the historical situation in ancient Yehud which may (or may not) underlie this passage might have been different. The ability to lend money does not necessarily make a person rich, and the cancellation of debt might have forced the debtors to pawn their own property. The fact that Nehemiah was able to cancel the debt does not inevitably mean that everyone was able to do so. We may also want to know who actually paid for the meals of the 150 people (cf. Grabbe 1998: 47).

The section ends in v. 19 with Nehemiah's plea to God: 'Remember for my good, O my God, all that I have done for this people.' This statement and others like it (cf. Neh. 13.14, 22, 31) have a mixed reception in history. Is it okay for Nehemiah to laud himself in this manner? (ch. 5)

Due to the reference to a later time, this section was either composed sometime after the building of the wall, or – if we maintain authorial unity – the entire Nehemiah Memoir is a later composition.

Nehemiah 6.1-14, 15-19; 7.1-5a

Synopsis

The next section begins in Neh. 6.1-14 with the declaration that the wall is finished and that, when hearing this, the three antagonists Sanballat, Tobiah and Geshem seek to meet with Nehemiah. Nehemiah, however, refuses to come as he understands the invitation to mean that the men wanted to do him harm. The fifth time they ask for a meeting, their request is accompanied by a letter which accuses Nehemiah of planning a rebellion against the Persian crown. Nehemiah denies the accusations and strengthens his resolve to complete the building process. Later, when Nehemiah visits a man called Shemaiah, the latter pleads with Nehemiah to hide, lest he be killed. Nehemiah again refuses to listen and concludes that Shemaiah is not to be trusted, as he is probably in the hire of Tobiah and Sanballat (maybe so that they could accuse him of cowardice). Nehemiah further mentions other people, among them Noadiah the prophetess, who are set to discredit and intimidate him.

Issues

Again, we need to remember that we only have Nehemiah's account. Looking at the issue historically, it is not unlikely that Nehemiah reported actual threats and his interpretation of them. There is, of course, another side of the story which is not represented. On a literary level, Nehemiah portrays himself as being a shrewd man who is able to see through lies easily, as well as being a brave man who refuses to hide away in times of danger but instead is resolved to see his projects through to the very end.

This is the first and only time that the prophetess Noadiah appears. She functions in the wider text of Ezra-Nehemiah as a counterpart to Haggai and Zechariah. While the latter two prophets supported the protagonists Joshua and Zerubbabel, Noadiah (as well as Shemaiah) are in the service of Nehemiah's enemies. This reference opens up a can of worms: to what extent was a prophet's word unmediated by social and political matters? The best parallel example comes from Jer. 28.1-17 which portrays the two prophets Jeremiah and Hananiah as having diametrically opposite words from God. It is also notable that Noadiah is a woman, both from a historical perspective (there were clearly female prophets in ancient Israel) and from a literary perspective (while the 'good' prophets Haggai and Zechariah are men, the 'bad' prophet is a woman).

Synopsis

In vv. 15-16, Nehemiah declares that the wall was finished. The people of Yehud, including their enemies, were astonished and realized that this was God's work.

Verses 17-19 are presented as a bit of an appendix. Verse 17 begins with 'in those days' which in its present context refers back to the day (sg.) when the wall was being finished, but it is also possible that this is a more general remark. Nehemiah writes that 'many of the Judean noblemen' were corresponding with Tobiah, that Tobiah was the son-in-law of Shecaniah, the son of Arah, and that this correspondence praised Tobiah in Nehemiah's presence. Nehemiah concludes by stating that he received threatening letters from Tobiah.

Issues

The passage in Neh. 6.17-19 suggests that Tobiah had close family connections with one of the leading priestly families in Yehud at the time. This impression is later confirmed by Neh. 13.4, which states that the priest

Eliashib was allied with Tobiah. Furthermore, although the name Shecaniah does not appear elsewhere in Ezra-Nehemiah, his father's name Arah is mentioned in the list of returned exiles in Ezra 2.5/7.10. This again raises the question of the unity/disunity of the community in Yehud at the time of Nehemiah. The exact identity of the 'Judean noblemen' is unclear yet again it is evident that these men were not wholehearted supporters of Nehemiah's projects.

Synopsis

The narrative about the wall continues in Neh. 7.1-5a. Nehemiah appoints his brother Hananiah to be in charge of Jerusalem and sets regulations as to when the city gates should be open and closed. He also notes the regrettably small population of the city, a statement which agrees with current archaeological findings (ch. 3), and thus decides to assemble the extant population in order to take a census.

Nehemiah 7.5b-73 [Heb. 7.5-72]

Synopsis

In Neh. 7.5b, Nehemiah states how he found genealogical records of those exiles who had arrived in Yehud early in the post-monarchic era. This statement fits well as the continuation of the previous section. Then follows a list of names and professions (vv. 6-72 [Heb. 6-71]), as well as a statement that they all settled into their towns (v. 73a [Heb. 72a]).

Issues

As noted above, this list also appears in Ezra 2. The main question, important for the reconstruction of the gradual growth of the text of Ezra-Nehemiah, concerns whether its original setting is located in Ezra or Nehemiah (ch. 2).

What is also unclear is the original setting of and thus the meaning of the statement in Neh. 7.73b [Heb. 72b]/Ezra 3.1a about the people being settled in their towns in the seventh month. Does this statement belong with the continuation in Ezra 3.2 and refer to the time of Joshua and Zerubbabel, or does it rather belong with the continuation in Nehemiah 8 and to the time of Ezra (and Nehemiah, see below)?

The appearance of this list in Nehemiah 7 also raises questions pertaining to the flow of the narrative. None of the matters noted in the list, that is, the names, occupations and area of settlement of the returnees, are taken up in the following Nehemiah 8. Instead, readers have to wait until Nehemiah 11 before the narrative returns to the issue of the population of Jerusalem and Yehud. On a broader scale, it is also important to note that the issue about the building of the walls of Jerusalem, which has been the key topic of Neh. 1–6 (7), is not going to appear again until Nehemiah 13. This 'gap' has significant repercussions for the way that we understand the composition history of Ezra-Nehemiah (ch. 2).

Nehemiah 8–10

The next main section in Ezra-Nehemiah is Neh. 8–10. These three chapters together portray the occasion of Ezra's reading of the Law and its aftermath. There is no main character in this section, yet Ezra and the Levites play significant roles. The main issue may be captured in one word: the Law/Torah itself.

Nehemiah 8.1-18

Synopsis

Neh. 8.1 continues straight on from the preceding verse that [in the seventh month] the people had gathered near the Water Gate. There is, however, a marked change. Nehemiah 8 is written in the third person and Nehemiah is no longer the narrator. In fact, although he figures briefly in v. 9, he does not have a speaking role in the chapter. Instead, Ezra 'the scribe', a person we have not encountered since Ezra 10, reappears with the 'book of the Instruction of Moses' (i.e. the Torah of Moses). Ezra remains as a literary persona throughout the chapter. The people request his presence, he stands on a pulpit before them surrounded by men, he reads the law for them, and he tells them that as the day is consecrated to God, so they should go and eat and drink and also send portions to those who do not have anything prepared.

The gathering continues a second day and the heads of the 'ancestral houses', all the people, the priests and the Levites come together to study the stipulations of the Law. When doing so, they realize that they ought to celebrate *Sukkoth* (the Feast of Tabernacles) and immediately begin to prepare for the holiday. The narrator notes that the people of Israel had not celebrated *Sukkoth* since the days of Joshua. Now, it is being celebrated for seven days, and the 'book of the Law of God' is being recited every day.

The Levites play an important role in this narrative. They are the ones who instruct the people (v. 9), who calm the people when they are agitated, and who are studying the Law.

Issues

Nehemiah 8 has caused a lot of consternation among readers. What is Ezra doing here? We have not heard about him for seven chapters and suddenly it becomes clear that he is a contemporary with Nehemiah and that they are working together! Furthermore, what is Nehemiah doing here, referred to in the third person, after six chapters of first-person speech? This abnormality, combined with the fact that he plays no active part in Nehemiah 8, has caused many scholars to assume that the name Nehemiah is a later addition to the text, added in order to create the impression that the two leaders were contemporaneous (ch. 2).

Another major scholarly concern relates to the content and character of the 'book of the law of Moses'. Is this the Pentateuch as we know it today, an earlier and less complete version of it, or only a part (such as the Priestly Source)? What is clear is that this Law must contain a description of *Sukkoth* (Lev. 23.33-44; Num. 29.12-40), otherwise the narrative does not work. At the same time, there are clear differences between the description of the celebration in Nehemiah 8 and that in the cultic calendar in the Pentateuch. For example, Nehemiah 8 does not mention *Yom Kippur* (which should have taken place four days prior to *Sukkoth* according to Lev. 16.29-34; 23.26-32; Num. 29.7-11) (ch. 3).

The notion in Neh. 8.8 that Ezra and the Levites 'explained' the 'book of Law' has given rise to the rabbinic tradition that Ezra here translated the Hebrew text of the Law into Aramaic, that is, the language that the returning exiles would have spoken while in Babylon. At the same time, there is no historical foundation to the claim that Hebrew was not the spoken language of Yehud which, in turn, renders it unlikely that the people in Jerusalem would have needed a translation (Grabbe 1998: 53). The notion of Ezra 'translating' the text has nevertheless become 'the founding legend' of the Aramaic *targumim* (the translations of the Hebrew Bible into Aramaic) (ch. 5).

Nehemiah 9.1-5

Synopsis

The following passage, also narrated in the third person, tells how the Israelites gathered together for a fast on the twenty-fourth day of the same month, when they confessed their sins. Those of Israelite descent separated themselves from those of foreign descent (v. 2). The Levites were again fulfilling an important role in this ceremony.

Issues

If this passage follows on directly from Nehemiah 8, there would only be one day between the end of the celebration of *Sukkoth* and this fast. Nehemiah 8 and 9 have a slightly different feel to them, though. While Nehemiah 8 speaks about all the people (Neh. 8.1), Neh. 9.1-5 states that the Israelites separated themselves from the foreigners (Neh. 9.2). These matters have led several scholars to detach Neh. 9.1-5 from the preceding Nehemiah 8 and to find a different original place for it, such as after Ezra 9–10 or before Neh. 13.1-3. Looking at the issue from the opposite direction, why a fast *now*? As mentioned above, the cultic calendar in the Pentateuch has *Yom Kippur* scheduled four days before *Sukkoth*. Why fasting *after* the festival and not before?

There is also some kind of incongruence between Neh. 9.2 and Ezra 9–10. Attentive readers begin to wonder: did they not divorce the foreign women already at the end of Ezra 10? If one reads Ezra-Nehemiah sequentially, readers are bound to think that whatever happened thirteen years earlier, it cannot have been very effective if it had to be repeated again now.

The solution to both problems may be to see Neh. 9.1-5 as a separate text which is connected to neither the Ezra tradition nor the Nehemiah tradition (Grabbe 1998: 55).

Nehemiah 9.6-37

Synopsis

Nehemiah 9.6-37 contains a long penitential prayer, uttered in the first person plural. It begins with a long overview of Israel's history (vv. 6-31), followed by a description of the community's present plight (vv. 32-37). This prayer draws extensively on earlier biblical texts. The historical overview can be subdivided into six smaller sections: Creation (v. 6), Ancestors (vv. 7-8), Exodus (vv. 9-11), Wilderness (vv. 12-21), Conquest (vv. 22-25) and Rebellion (presumably during the time of the Judges (vv. 26-31) (Blenkinsopp 1988: 303–6).

Issues

This prayer raises literary and historical questions that to a large extent are interrelated. First, was this prayer composed for the purpose of illustrating the people's penitence in Neh. 9.1-5, or did the prayer originate outside the Ezra-Nehemiah traditions and was added to its present context only secondarily? While the prayer fits well in the present narrative context, nothing in it is tied to the specific situation in Yehud in the fifth century BCE. On the contrary, the description of the people's situation in vv. 32-37 does not mention the issue of intermarriages (Ezra 9–10) and it only refers to the Law in very general terms (v. 34). The people are being enslaved in their own land (v. 36) and its produce goes to kings whom God has placed upon them (v. 37). This description does not agree with the positive (and always nuanced) depiction of the (Persian) kings elsewhere in Ezra-Nehemiah. Finally, the absence of any reference to the exile is notable and does not suit the notion that the people praying are from among the returnees (ch. 2).

These points have led several scholars to postulate an earlier date to this prayer. In addition, a few exegetes see it as an expression of the people who had remained in the land (Williamson 1988; Tiemeyer 2008). Other scholars argue in favour of coherence with the rest of Ezra-Nehemiah and thus see Nehemiah 9 as being composed and selected by the main editors of Ezra-Nehemiah to express key themes of the book as a whole (Eskenazi 2001).

Nehemiah 9.38–10.39 [Heb. 10.1-40]

Synopsis

The opening statement in Neh. 9.38 [Heb. 10.1], uttered in the first person plural (but it is unclear who the speakers are), appears to refer back to the prayer in Nehemiah 9. Then a long list of names of the leaders, the priests and the Levites (vv. 1-27 [Heb. vv. 2-28]) follows. Heading the list is Nehemiah, the governor while there is no mention of Ezra. Verse 28 [Heb. v. 29] mentions the rest of the people, specified as the priests, Levites, gatekeepers, singers, temple servants and all those who separated themselves from the people of the nations.

Issues

Verse 28 [Heb. v. 29] is somewhat incongruous with the preceding list in vv. 1-27, as that list already singled out the priests and the Levites. Instead, v. 28 fits better as the direct continuation of the opening statement in Neh. 9.38 (Blenkinsopp 1988: 314). The continuity with v. 38 and the incongruity between v. 1 and v. 28 together suggest, on the one hand, that Neh. 9.38; 10.28-39 is one narrative and, on the other hand, that the list in Neh. 10.1-27 is of independent origin and was inserted into the narrative at a later stage in the development of the text (ch. 2).

Synopsis

Verses 29-39 [Heb. vv. 30-40] state that these people, with their families, pledged to follow the Law: (1) not to intermarry; (2) not to trade on the Sabbath; (3) to let the land rest every seventh year; (4) to support the temple sacrificial cult; and (5) to bring all first fruits to the temple.

Issues

These pledges agree on a general basis with what has happened earlier in the text of Ezra-Nehemiah, yet they would fit better *after* the events which are told in Nehemiah 13 (dealing with Sabbath observance and intermarriage). It is therefore likely that Nehemiah 10, indeed all of Neh. 8–10 (see above, Nehemiah 8), is not part of NM and instead forms an editorial subsection which in all likelihood is later than the material in Neh. 1–6 (7) (ch. 2).

Nehemiah 11–13

The last three chapters of the book of Nehemiah constitute the fifth and final main section of Ezra-Nehemiah. Like the preceding Neh. 8–10, it is not a homogenous whole but consists of several, probably originally independent subsections. Unlike the preceding sections, the material in Neh. 11–13 appears to be a somewhat haphazard collection of texts with no clear kernel, yet offering insight into the situation of the people in Yehud, their settlements and their occupations. At the same time, it is fair to say, at least from a historical perspective, that the key event is the dedication of the temple described in Neh. 12.27–13.3.

Nehemiah 11.1-24, 25-36; 12.1-26

Synopsis

Neh. 11.1 begins by stating that the leaders of the people were living in Jerusalem. The rest of the people stayed in the rural areas and in other cities. In order to remedy the situation of an underpopulated Jerusalem, the people cast lots and decided that every tenth man would settle in Jerusalem (v. 2).

Verses 3-19 list the names of the people who had volunteered to settle in Jerusalem in accordance with their tribal affiliation: Judah, Benjamin and Levi, the latter group being further subdivided according to profession: priests, Levites and gatekeepers. Verse 20 continues to describe the population in the wider Yehud. The rest of the people lived in the towns of Yehud, each in their ancestral plot. Verses 21-24 become more specific again as they mention the names of particular men in charge of different groups of cultic personnel, as well as singling out Pethahiah son of Meshezabel as the king's advisor.

Issues

This text opens up the question of the actual size of Jerusalem in the fifth century BCE. Why was there a need to ask for volunteers to settle in the city? After all, it was the old capital and the place of the temple. Would that not make it an attractive place? We shall discuss the historical situation of Yehud in the fifth century BCE, as well as the more specific question of the demography of Yehud, in ch. 3.

It also brings up literary questions. In particular, how does a decimated population in Jerusalem fit the description of Jerusalem and the rebuilding of the wall in the preceding parts of Ezra-Nehemiah? In the case of Neh. 1–6, there is no overt contradiction in the sense that Nehemiah, being one of the leaders, would naturally have dwelt in Jerusalem. At the same time, did the other people mentioned in Neh. 1–6 travel to Jerusalem for business? This statement also fits with the impression given in Ezra 9–10 where the people journey to Jerusalem to be part of Ezra's convocation, yet plead with him to be able to go home to their own towns because of the rain (Ezra 10.12-15).

Synopsis

Neh. 11.25-36 continues with another list, this time featuring the names of the settlements. The listed place names are organized in two groups: Judahite locations and Benjamite locations.

Issues

This list has several strange features. First, from a literary perspective, many of these place names are never mentioned elsewhere in Ezra-Nehemiah. Secondly, from a historical perspective, some locations (e.g. Kiriath-arba) were not part of Yehud in the fifth century BCE, but instead under Edomite-Arab control (Blenkinsopp 1988: 328–9). This situation has caused scholars to explore the allusions to other texts that these places convey, in particularly to the book of Joshua. It is possible that, in alluding to these place names, this list serves to create an impression that Yehud was settled in accordance to the same pattern as the one that Joshua used after the Exodus (Blenkinsopp 1988: 330, see further ch. 2).

Neh. 12.1-26 features yet a third list or rather a set of lists, this time enumerating the temple personnel with focus on priests and Levites. The earliest list itemizes those who came to Yehud at the same time as Joshua and Zerubbabel (cf. Ezra 2–6). Another list catalogues the sequence of High Priests, concluding with Joshua's decedent Jaddua (5 generations).

Nothing prevents us from assigning different dates to the different lists in this passage. At the same time, the reference to Jaddua provides an effective *terminus post quem*, that is, the earliest possible date of compilation of Neh. 12.1-26. As such, it can also tell us something about the date of compilation of the entire Ezra-Nehemiah. It cannot be earlier than the late fourth century BCE, and it may be later than Alexander the Great. As a result, Ezra-Nehemiah in its current form is the product of the Hellenistic period (Blenkinsopp 1988: 334).

Nehemiah 12.27-43

Synopsis

Neh. 12.27-43 catapults the reader back to Nehemiah and to the rebuilding of the wall. This passage, narrated in the first person singular (presumably Nehemiah but this is never stated) tells how the Levites were in charge of the dedication of the wall, accompanied by singers and musicians coming from all around Jerusalem. The priests and the Levites purified themselves, the people, the wall   and the gates. The narrator led the leaders up upon the wall where they proceeded in two groups and in opposite directions while making music. The rejoicing of the people could be heard from afar. Verse 33 mentions the name Ezra alongside several other names.

Issues

This passage is not dated. It is natural to read it as the continuation of Neh. 1–6, that is, as an event which took place during Nehemiah's first year in Jerusalem. This raises questions about the current location of the text. What role does it fill in its present position? It is possible that the compiler wished to delay reporting about the dedication of the wall until the end of the book (Grabbe 1998: 62). It can be read as part of NM, yet as the first-person narrator is never specified, this is not the only possible reading of the final form.

If this text is being read as uttered by Nehemiah, and if one assumes that the man Ezra mentioned in v. 33 is the narrator of Ezra 7–10, then this is the only other text beside Nehemiah 8 that features both leaders at the same time. Eskenazi, for example, reads the final form of the text as implying that Ezra and Nehemiah lead the two processions (Eskenazi 1988: 116). Understood in this way, Neh. 12.27-43 is clearly not only the heart but also the climax of all of Ezra-Nehemiah (ch. 2).

There are some peculiar aspects to this ceremony. First, the lack of references to the reading of the Law and the pledge by the community to fulfil that Law (Neh. 8–10) is odd, given that both matters would have been relevant at the time of the ceremony (Grabbe 1998: 62). Second, the manner of the dedication of the wall is surprising. Why is the city wall being treated as if it were a sacred object? As Grabbe points out, this passage brings to mind the dedication of the temple as narrated in Ezra 6.15-17 (Grabbe 1998: 63).

Nehemiah 12.44-47

Synopsis

The short section in Neh. 12.44-47 speaks of the organization of the tithes and other contributions to the temple and of their storage. It also states that the priests and Levites performed to everyone's satisfaction and, as a result, the cult of Yhwh ran smoothly as in the golden days of King David. The section also mentions the more recent time of Nehemiah and Zerubbabel.

Issues

This section is loosely connected with the preceding passage through the phrase 'on that day' which in the present text must refer to the day when the wall was being dedicated. Yet, it is clear from the reference to Nehemiah, alongside Zerubbabel, that this is not the integral continuation of Nehemiah's first-person report in Neh. 12.27-43. The combined reference to Nehemiah and Zerubbabel is also surprising, given the view elsewhere in Ezra-Nehemiah that they were not contemporaries. Was one or the other or both names added to this section secondarily (ch. 2)?

Nehemiah 13.1-3

Synopsis

The next section in Neh. 13.1-3 speaks about the reading of the 'book of Moses' and the discovery that it proclaims the ban on Ammonites and Moabites from entering God's congregation. As a result of this discovery, all people of mixed descent were being separated from Israel.

Issues

This section also begins with the phrase 'on that day'. If the passage is read sequentially in its current context, the phrase refers to events which took place on the day when the wall was being dedicated. At the same time, its content relates more to the material in Neh. 8–10, as well as to the material in Ezra 9–10. The text from the 'book of Moses' that is being referred to is presumably Deut. 23.4-7 (Eng. vv. 3-6) which bans Ammonites and Moabites from God's congregation (ch. 3).

Nehemiah 13.4-14

Synopsis

Neh. 13.4-14 brings us back again to Nehemiah's first-person narrative. Nehemiah tells how Eliashib had abused his position of being in charge of the storerooms of the temple by allocating a large room for himself which really should have been used for storage of material related to the sacrificial cult. Eliashib, the reader is further being informed, is a relative of Tobiah, one of the three antagonists of Neh. 1–6. Oddly enough, this room seems to have contained Tobiah's belongings rather than those of Eliashib. We also learn that Eliashib's abuse of the system had happened in Nehemiah's absence. Nehemiah had been recalled (to Susa) in the thirty-second year of Artaxerxes' reign. Now, however, Nehemiah has received royal permission to return to Jerusalem. He is back and, seeing the neglect of the temple, he acts. He throws out Tobiah's belongings from the storeroom and brings back the cultic vessels. Furthermore, upon learning that the Levites have not received their salaries and, presumably as a result, have returned home alongside the musicians, Nehemiah brings them back. He also restores the tithings and appoints new temple personnel.

Issues

The section in Neh. 13.4 begins with the phrase 'before this'. Reading the text sequentially, the section speaks about events recounted in Neh. 13.1-3 about the segregation (above). At the same time, as v. 6 informs us, Nehemiah has been away for some time. Based on the information in Neh. 5.14, Nehemiah had been twelve years in Jerusalem (cf. Neh. 5.14) before he left. This brings us up to at least the thirty-second year of Artaxerxes' reign, that is, to 433–432 BCE (ch. 2).

The matter about the Levites can be understood as a simple case of neglect. Alternatively, this narrative may allude to a case of rivalry between different cultic groups in Yehud (priests *versus* Levites) (Grabbe 1998: 65).

Nehemiah 13.15-22

Synopsis

In Neh. 13.15-22, Nehemiah continues to describe his reforms, this time relating to Sabbath observance. Nehemiah narrates how he saw people working and trading on the Sabbath and how he, in order to rectify the situation, commanded that the city gates be closed and guarded on the Sabbath so that no produce could be brought into the city.

Issues

The section begins with the clause 'in those days', which lends a flavour of reminiscence to the narrative. It also makes it uncertain when exactly Nehemiah observed these matters.

The narrative in Neh. 13.15-22 brings the story in Jer. 17.19-27 to mind where God forbade the people from carrying a load and bringing it through the city gates on the Sabbath. Such a ban is a very stringent interpretation of the Sabbath laws in Exod. 20.8-11 and Deut. 5.12-15 (Blenkinsopp 1988: 359). The importance of the Sabbath for the post-monarchic community is also confirmed by passages such as Isa. 56.1-8 and 58.13 (ch. 3).

Nehemiah 13.23-31

Synopsis

The last section in Ezra-Nehemiah is devoted to Nehemiah's dealings with mixed marriages. Nehemiah observes that Jewish men had married women from Ashdod, Ammon and Moab and that the couples' children did not speak Hebrew. Nehemiah proceeds by remonstrating with them, cursing them, striking some of the men and pulling out their hair, and making them swear an oath to God to stop marrying foreign women and also to stop giving their daughters to foreign men. He further banished a priest who had married one of Sanballat's daughters. Given this defilement of the priesthood, Nehemiah purifies the priests and sets up guidelines for the priests and the Levites. He also sorts out matters relating to the sacrificial cult.

Issues

This passage raises a series of questions from both a literary and a historical perspective. Why did Nehemiah encounter mixed marriages? Did not Ezra already deal with this issue in Ezra 9–10 (presuming that Ezra preceded Nehemiah or that the text of Ezra 7–10 preceded the text of Nehemiah 13)? From a moral view-point, how can we relate to Nehemiah's actions? He is portrayed as an extremely harsh and temperamental man who lacks compassion, who treats foreigners badly and who breaks up marriages (ch. 4). Finally, it is worth noting that the scroll of Ezra-Nehemiah as a whole ends on a somewhat sour and open-ended note. Intermarriages are dangerous; nevertheless the people of Yehud keep marrying outside of the community.

Bibliography

Key monographs

Eskenazi, Tamara Cohn. *In an Age of Prose: A Literary Approach to Ezra-Nehemiah* (SBLMS, 36: Atlanta, GA: Scholars Press, 1988).
Grabbe, Lester L. *Ezra-Nehemiah* (Old Testament Readings; London and New York: Routledge, 1998).

Key commentaries

Blenkinsopp, Joseph. *Ezra-Nehemiah* (OTL; Philadelphia, PA: Westminster Press, 1988).
Williamson, H. G. M. *Ezra-Nehemiah* (WBC, 16; Waco, TX: Word Books, 1985).

2

The Composition History
of Ezra-Nehemiah

We noted in ch. 1 that Ezra-Nehemiah contains a variety of different documents and styles. In this chapter, we shall explore how these different texts came to be incorporated into the text that we have before us. Given the diversity that we have seen so far, as well as the changing narrative voice, it is clear that Ezra-Nehemiah is the result of extensive editorial work. One person, or more likely a series of people, gathered the various texts together and strove to create a coherent whole.

In ch. 1, we identified five main sections in Ezra-Nehemiah: Ezra 1–6; 7–10; Neh. 1–7; 8–10; and 11–13, and observed that each section is loosely held together by a shared main topic. At the same time, we also noticed that several passages in Ezra-Nehemiah are mutually contradictory. These discrepancies, combined with changes in theme, style and narrative voice, have led scholars to suggest a plethora of different models for the composition of Ezra-Nehemiah; here I shall highlight some of the more influential ones.

When looking at the compositional history of Ezra-Nehemiah, there are two main ways of imagining the editorial process: (1) to see it as the compilation of documents that to a large degree existed independently, prior to their incorporation into Ezra-Nehemiah; or (2) to see the text as a composition that gradually grew, where later authors added material to one original text. The following discussion will not distinguish too rigidly between these two types of models, especially since many models contain aspects of both, yet it is important to bear the difference in mind. The discussion will be based on and guided by some of the issues raised in the preceding chapter. For reasons that will soon become apparent, the sections will be discussed in the following order: Ezra 1–6; 7–10; Neh. 1–6; 13; Neh. 8–10; Neh. 11–12.

Many of the recent redaction-critical theories (i.e. theories which focus on how editors/redactors have shaped the source material to express their own theological goals) understand the formation of Ezra and Nehemiah to be intertwined, and argue in favour of a shared process of creation across the two books. There are, however, several strong voices in favour of seeing two distinct editorial processes, whereby Ezra developed as a book independently from Nehemiah, or at least in parallel (e.g. Becking 1999). VanderKam, for example, highlights linguistic features that are unique to each of the two books (VanderKam 1992), while Kraemer emphasizes the differences in their ideology (Kraemer 1993). In contrast, other scholars argue equally strongly in favour of their overall unity (e.g. Duggan 2001: 35–7; Eskenazi 1988: 11–14). In my view, the differences in vocabulary and ideology are best explained by postulating independent textual blocks that were later fused together by the editors responsible for the creation of the Ezra-Nehemiah scroll. These editors also added material in order to create a (somewhat) coherent whole with a (somewhat) unified message across both books.

Ezra 1–6

Ezra 1–6 is a compilation consisting of various types of material. Readers encounter lists, letters and narratives that are dated to different time periods and to the reigns of different monarchs. Are these letters and edicts authentic historical records which the editors copied into the text of Ezra-Nehemiah in the same way as writers today would quote and annotate earlier texts to which they refer? Alternatively, could these letters be fictional in the sense that the editors wrote them to illustrate their point? The same questions are relevant also when we look at the lists, both in Ezra 1–6 and elsewhere in Ezra-Nehemiah. Furthermore, what is the chronological relationship between Ezra 1–6 on the one hand, and the rest of the material in Ezra-Nehemiah on the other?

Ezra 1–6 as a textual unit

Despite the fact that Ezra 1–6 contains diverse documents, some of which may have been purpose-written for their current place in Ezra-Nehemiah (i.e. for their *Sitz in der Literatur*) and some may be authentic documents that were incorporated (and potentially also reworked) into their present context by an editor, the fact remains that Ezra 1–6 forms some kind of textual unit. The question is: what is the character and message of that unit?

Chronologically, Ezra 1–6 stretches from 539 BCE when Cyrus came to power in Babylon (Ezra 1.1) until the sixth year of Darius' reign when the temple was rebuilt (Ezra 5.16). Assuming that this is Darius I (522–486 BCE) (an assumption supported by the account in Haggai and Zechariah), the year is 515 BCE. Interspersed are also letters from the subsequent reign of Artaxerxes.

The main topic of Ezra 1–6 is the rebuilding of the temple. In view of this, some scholars have identified this text as a 'temple building story', that is, a genre of literature, common to the ancient Near East, which describes the destruction of the temple by foreign forces and its triumphant rebuilding. Although the material in Ezra 1–6 does not comprise a simple temple building story, it features all the expected main building blocks: a commissioning to rebuild the temple; the acquisition and preparation of building material; the laying of the foundation; references to subsequent key points in the building works; a statement that the king has built the temple; and the dedication ceremony (Fried 2010: 328–38).

Ezra 1–6 also has a unique collection of dramatis personae who do not appear later on in EM and NM, most pertinently Sheshbazzar, Zerubbabel and Joshua from among the returning exiles. The first two men are associated with the rebuilding of the temple in Jerusalem: Sheshbazzar is portrayed as laying the foundation of the temple during the reign of Cyrus, and Zerubbabel is portrayed as being involved in its completion during the reign of Darius I twenty-two years later (although Zerubbabel famously is not mentioned in Ezra 5.16, see ch. 5).

The authenticity of the edicts and the letters

Ezra 1–6 contains a number of documents:

- Cyrus's Edict (Ezra 1.1-4), written in Hebrew
- A letter to Artaxerxes (Ezra 4.8-16), written in Aramaic
- Artaxerxes's reply (Ezra 4.17-22), written in Aramaic
- A letter from Tattenai and Shethar-bozenai to Darius (Ezra 5.7-17), written in Aramaic
- Cyrus's Edict (Ezra 6.2-5), written in Aramaic
- Darius's reply (Ezra 6.6-12), written in Aramaic

In addition, Ezra 7.12-26 features Artaxerxes's decree to Ezra, written in Aramaic.

The authenticity of these letters has preoccupied many scholars. Does the biblical text cite actual letters or are these letters fictitious? There are, as Grabbe highlights in his substantial investigation of the biblical documents, four general issues that need to be considered:

1   No document in Aramaic from the entire Persian Empire resembles the documents embedded in the biblical texts. We therefore do not have a firm basis for comparisons.
2   The type of Aramaic that is used in the biblical document differs from the Imperial Aramaic that is employed in Aramaic documents from the Persian period. They show elements of both Imperial Aramaic and later Middle Aramaic. If the biblical documents are genuine, we need to assume that the biblical scribes 'updated' the language and the spelling (orthography) to fit later usages.
3   The epistolary formulas (i.e. formulas used in letters for greetings etc.) in the biblical letters disagree with those in other Persian period letters. Instead, they show affinity with letters written in the early Hellenistic age. As above, if the biblical letters are authentic, we must assume that they have been edited at a later date.

4   The content of the letters is not in line with the Persian attitude
towards temples and cults displayed in other material, as the
Persians in no other case offered financial support or granted tax
concessions to local cultic endeavours (cf. ch. 3).

Grabbe concludes that the biblical documents are unlikely to be authentic
in their present form. It should also be acknowledged that the biblical
material testifies to a large degree to Jewish theology (i.e. references to
Yhwh and Israel, as well as lack of references to the governor and other
imperial appointees). It further has distinct nuances of propaganda: the
king makes a decision in favour of Yehud, without consulting his substantial
administrative apparatus consisting of satraps and local governors, and he
shows blatant favouritism towards the Jerusalem temple (Grabbe 2006).

In view of the comparative non-biblical material, we can either conclude
that the editors of Ezra-Nehemiah used authentic letters but updated their
language and style to fit their own (later) conventions, or that the letters are
fictitious from beginning to end, composed in order to emphasize a key
feature of the narrative. The latter view is the most extreme option; there is,
however, some middle ground. Grabbe himself opts for a compromise in
that he envisions a spectrum of authenticity, with some of the documents
reflecting a higher degree of authenticity than others. For example, he argues
that Tattenai's letter in Ezra 5.7-17 contains the most authentic material
while Cyrus's edict in Hebrew in Ezra 1.2-4 contains very little, if any,
genuine material (Grabbe 2006: 562–3). We may therefore conclude that the
editors of Ezra-Nehemiah had some genuine documents at their disposal,
which they reworked to fit their own theological claim that the Persian
authority gave its full support to Sheshbazzar, Zerubbabel and Joshua as they
endeavoured to re-establish Jerusalem as a cultic centre with a functioning
temple in its midst.

The lists in Ezra 1–6 and beyond

Ezra-Nehemiah contains multiple lists of people and settlements. In their
current literary context, they function as following:

- Ezra 2.1-67/Neh. 7.6-67 contains a list of Babylonian exiles who
  arrived in Yehud under the leadership of Joshua and Zerubbabel.
- Ezra 8.1, 2-14 enumerates the people and their extended families who
  arrived in Yehud from Babylon together with Ezra.

- Ezra 10.18-44 lists the men who had married foreign women during the time of Ezra.
- Neh. 3.1-32 provides details of the people who were involved in the building of the city wall around Jerusalem during the time of Nehemiah.
- Neh. 10.1-28 [Eng. 9.38–10.27] numbers the people who sealed an agreement with Nehemiah.
- Neh. 11.1-24 catalogues the people who settled in Yehud.
- Neh. 11.25-36 records the settlements in the areas of Yehud and Benjamin.
- Neh. 12.1-26 registers the cultic officials who returned with Zerubbabel and Joshua.

In a similar way as with the above-mentioned letters and edicts, these lists raise questions pertaining to the composition of Ezra-Nehemiah. Are they external compositions that an editor chose to incorporate into his work, or are they his own compositions, written in order to lend a sense of historicity to the narrative? If the former, is it possible that the individual lists had an original function which was lost when they were incorporated into Ezra-Nehemiah?

In their present literary context, these lists have multiple roles. They fill a literary function according to Angel. The list in Ezra 2, for instance, gives the impression that a large number of people returned to Yehud, despite the historical fact that most Jews remained in Babylon (Angel 2007: 144–5). They may also provide structure to the narrative. For Eskenazi, the list in Ezra 2/Nehemiah 7 serves as an *inclusio* (a literary device which frames a given text by placing similar material at its beginning and its end) around the central part of the narrative (see further below) (Eskenazi 1988: 182).

The list in Ezra 2/Nehemiah 7

The fact that one of these lists, namely, the list in Ezra 2.1-67, appears also in Neh. 7.6-67, plays a pivotal role in deciding the relative chronology of the various texts in Ezra-Nehemiah. Put succinctly, is the compilation of Ezra 1–6 earlier or later than the compilation of the Nehemiah material? With solid arguments on both sides of the debate, there is so far no consensus view.

Speaking in favour of Nehemiah 7 as the original place for the list, Williamson argues that the list is well integrated in its literary context in Nehemiah 7 and that Ezra 2 presupposes Nehemiah 7 in its current position.

Moreover, the list in Ezra 2 is an expanded yet also simplified version of the one in Nehemiah 7. First, the numbers in Ezra 2 are rounded off (cf. Ezra 2.68-69 *versus* Neh. 7.69-71), and second, Ezra 2.68 has no correspondence in the list in Nehemiah 7. It follows, so Williamson, that Ezra 2 (and all of Ezra 1–6) was composed at a time when the EM and the NM had already been combined (Williamson 1983: 2–4; 1985: xxxiv, 29–30). More recent scholars maintain, however, that Ezra 2 is the original place for the list (Grätz 2004: 35–8; Pakkala 2004: 137–40; Wright 2004: 301–3). Burt, for example, argues that Nehemiah 7 has modified the numbers in order to make the total number of immigrants come to ten times the numbers in the list in Neh. 11.14-19. He further suggests that neither of the two lists in Nehemiah is integral to the Nehemiah tradition but form later additions (Burt 2014: 58–61).

Ezra 1.1-3a and 2 Chronicles 36.22-23

The first two and a half verses in Ezra (vv. 1-3a) are identical with the last two verses in 2 Chronicles (36.22-23). This overlap has led to the common scholarly theory that the editor of 1–2 Chronicles ('the Chronicler') was also the editor of Ezra-Nehemiah. This theory is further bolstered by a certain degree of thematic, theological and linguistic affinity between the two sets of texts, as well as by the evidence from 1 Esdras which consists of 2 Chron. 35–36, all of Ezra, and Nehemiah 8 (see further below). 1 Esdras is a book written in Greek, which appears only in the Septuagint (LXX). It was probably composed in Alexandria in the early Ptolemaic period (323–200 BCE) (Fried 2014: 3).

This view has not gone unchallenged. Japhet, for example, has demonstrated that there are important stylistic differences between Ezra-Nehemiah on the one hand, and Chronicles on the other (Japhet 1968). Williamson follows suit, showing that although the two sets of texts treat similar themes and interests, this affinity is in itself insufficient to prove shared authorship. Speaking specifically about the overlap between 2 Chron. 36.22-23 and Ezra 1.1-3a, Williamson argues that the material is more likely to be original to Ezra and incorporated later into Chronicles than pointing to shared authorship. Furthermore, there are no reasons to assume that Ezra-Nehemiah and Chronicles at one point formed one textual sequence which later was subdivided (Williamson 1977: 7–11). Turning to 1 Esdras, Williamson views it as a secondary work which compiles and fuses together several textual sources that originally belonged apart. As such, 1 Esdras cannot be used to support common authorship of Ezra-Nehemiah and Chronicles (Williamson 1977: 35–6).

In response to these objections, yet more recent scholars have highlighted some methodological concerns with Japhet's and Williamson's claims. Blenkinsopp, for example, notes that given the extensive use of sources in Ezra-Nehemiah, it is difficult to carry out linguistic and stylistic investigations. Blenkinsopp further maintains that this type of investigation cuts both ways, as it is not only possible to highlight a distinct vocabulary but also a shared vocabulary, which in this case is a significant amount (Blenkinsopp 1988: 47–54). Redditt likewise postulates that the editor of Ezra-Nehemiah drew on and also alluded to material unique to Chronicles. This 'borrowing' makes the editing of Ezra-Nehemiah later than the compilation of Chronicles, but it does not, however, necessarily imply that the Chronicler edited Ezra-Nehemiah, but instead suggests that the two textual corpora were edited by different hands (Redditt 2008). From a different angle, Throntveit analyses Japhet's and Williamson's arguments and interacts with the claims of their opponents. He concludes that the linguistic evidence is not enough to provide certainty either way. In his view, though, our starting point should be that the editor of Ezra-Nehemiah is distinct from the Chronicler, in part because they appear as separate books in the Bible. The burden of proof thus rests in the hands of those who argue for common authorship, not vice versa (Throntveit 1982).

Ezra 7–10

Until fairly recently, the EM and the NM were considered to be internally consistent and thus treated as having been written by the two historical men: Ezra wrote his memoir and Nehemiah wrote his memoir. Today, however, this consensus has eroded and given way to different models according to which both memoirs are the result of gradual textual growth. In these discussions, it is important to differentiate between two modes of inquiry: historical questions and literary questions. These two types of question are not mutually exclusive, but they have to be kept apart for methodological reasons. In the present chapter, the question does not concern whether something happened or not (historically) but whether the narrative about the event is integral or not to the text in which it is now situated. Expressed differently, literary criticism is not concerned with the *Sitz im Leben* ('setting in life') of a given text, only in its *Sitz in der Literatur* ('setting in literature').

The special case of Nehemiah 8

What complicates the picture when studying Ezra 7–10 is Nehemiah 8. Only in this chapter (as well as a reference in the list in Neh. 12.26) do Ezra and Nehemiah appear together as dramatis personae. Moreover, they are being referred to in the third person, in contrast to their respective first-person narratives in Ezra 7–10 and Neh. 1–7, 13. These references pose the obvious question: what has Ezra been up to since we last encountered him (i.e. during the building of the wall), and why did he wait thirteen years to read the Law (i.e. the time between his arrival in Yehud in the seventh year [Ezra 7.8] and this reading in the twentieth year [Neh. 1.1])? Turning the problem upside down, what is Nehemiah doing here in Nehemiah 8? He lacks a speaking part and is merely referred to in Neh. 8.9 as 'governor', using the Aramaic title 'the tirshata' (cf. Ezra 2.63/Neh. 7.65, 69 [Eng. 2.70]; 10.2 [Eng. 10.3]). The reader may well wonder why he suddenly appears here in the third person with his title, after seven chapters of listening to his authorial voice (Grabbe 1998: 55).

These issues have caused a number of scholars to argue that Nehemiah 8 is really the direct continuation of Ezra 7–10. We may thus speak about an Ezra source that consists of three longer passages which refer to Ezra in the third person (7.1-10; 10.1-44; Neh. 8.1-18) and one long section which refers to Ezra in the first person (7.12–9.15). Alternatively, are we dealing with two sources – an EM and an Ezra narrative – or with one source? Neither the first nor the second set of texts constitutes a complete story in itself. The first lacks an adequate conclusion while the second lacks an adequate beginning. It can thus be argued that only the combination of the two sets of texts provides the whole story (Duggan 2001: 13–15).

The curious case of 1 Esdras

The above-mentioned 1 Esdras provides further support for an Ezra Source which consisted of Ezra 7–10 and Nehemiah 8. This book arranges the textual units in Ezra-Nehemiah in an order that is different from the one in the Masoretic Text (MT = the authoritative Hebrew [and Aramaic] text of the Hebrew Bible for Rabbinic Judaism). Of relevance here is the fact that

Neh. 7.72–8.13a follows directly after Ezra 10.44 and thus concludes the Ezra narrative.

There are two ways of reading Nehemiah 8 together with Ezra 7–10:

1   According to the order of 1 Esdras, the reading of the law (Nehemiah 8) forms the ceremonial *ratification* of the marriage reform (Ezra 9–10).

2   Alternatively, as many critical scholars do, it makes narrative sense to read Ezra 7–8; Nehemiah 8; Ezra 9–10. According to this reading, the reading of the law (Nehemiah 8) *triggered* the marriage crisis (Ezra 9–10) (Duggan 2001: 6–7).

1 Esdras is a compilation in the sense that it selects and combines material from various sources. At the same time, the question remains whether 1 Esdras at times testifies to an earlier *Vorlage* (i.e. an earlier version) of a given textual unit. Recently, a collection of articles edited by Lisbeth Fried has been devoted to the chronological question of 1 Esdras versus the canonical Ezra (i.e. the version in the MT) (Fried 2011). As can be expected, there is no consensus view. Many of the articles share the underlying principles that what is complex is later simplified and what is brief is later elaborated.

There are instances where the canonical Ezra contains the longer text (e.g. Ezra 4.6-11a vs. 1 Esdr. 2.15). Several scholars uphold the rule that the longer text often preserves a later, expanded version of the text. In this case, it would be more likely that the author/compiler of canonical Ezra offered a later, longer version than that the author/compiler of 1 Esdras deliberately condensed the source in front of him (Fulton and Knoppers 2011: 17, 24–5). Looking more at the structure of the two books, 1 Esdr. 2–7 has a complicated storyline which suggests two different, parallel versions, while the narrative in Ezra 2; 5–7 is relatively simple. Is it more feasible that someone took the two parallel versions (1 Esdras) and transformed them into one narrative (canonical Ezra) (Schenker 2011), or that the compiler of 1 Esdras wished to present a more fully fledged version of the less developed, earlier text in Ezra (Pakkala 2011)?

Much pivots on the presentation of Zerubbabel. The story of the three youths (1 Esdr. 3–4) appears only in 1 Esdras and not in the canonical Ezra. This story bears all the hallmarks of a Hellenistic court tale, along the same lines as Esther and Dan. 1–6. Did at one point an earlier version of 1 Esdras exist, which did not contain this story (Grabbe 1998: 72–3), or is the current form of 1 Esdras original in the sense that it never existed without this story (Becking 2011)? If the latter, it is likely (but not inevitable) that the present form of 1 Esdras is later than the canonical Ezra. Digging even deeper, it is worthwhile asking whether the story at one point was an independent traditional story or whether it was purpose-written for its current position in 1 Esdras.

In either case, the tale of the three youths in 1 Esdr. 3–4 is a later development of the traditions surrounding Zerubbabel. Its purpose in 1 Esdras is to give more prestige to Zerubbabel and to provide him with a suitable background (Talshir 2011: 113). It is, in fact, possible to relate to 1 Esdras as a commentary on the canonical Ezra. It increases the overall presence of Zerubbabel and it gives him additional credits (e.g. for bringing the holy vessels to Jerusalem alongside Sheshbazzar, 1 Esdr. 6.18) (VanderKam 2011).

As to why 1 Esdras was composed, many reasons favour seeing it as an example of 'rewritten Bible'. It is a free-standing composition, which replicates but does not supersede or replace the canonical book (Williamson 2011). More specifically, it provides a modified version of the restoration of Yehud which seeks to depict the period of the fall of Judah, the return from exiles, and the restoration of the community as a continuum which reached its climax with Ezra and his reading of the Law. This climax corresponded to the compiler's own reality where the political power rested with the Hellenistic rulers, while the local population of Jerusalem was governed by the High Priest (Japhet 2011). Ezra, seen in this way, is remodelled as 'the chief priest' (Wright 2004: 6).

Redaction-critical models for Ezra 7–10 and Nehemiah 8

Scholars have tried to explain the creation of the extant Ezra text in different ways. There are two main schools of thought. First, some scholars view the bulk of Ezra 7–10 and Nehemiah 8 as a first-person memoir, written by the historical person named Ezra. Williamson, for example, traces most of the material back to Ezra, while allowing for parts of the material to have been secondarily transformed into a third-person account by an editor (Williamson 1985: 147–49).

Alternatively, other scholars identify an original narrative about Ezra and subsequent textual layers. Pakkala, for instance, detects an early third-person narrative about Ezra and six later expansions, as well as several glosses and other unidentified and independent additions. Notably, Pakkala recognizes (an early form of) the narrative in Nehemiah 8 to be connected at the very earliest stage with the EM (Pakkala 2004: 301).

- The earliest text begins in Ezra 7.1, 6, 8, continues in Neh. 8.1-3, 9-10, 12a, and ends in Ezra 10.1-4, 10-14a and 16b-17. This brief account, narrated in the third person, tells the readers how Ezra arrived in Yehud in order to teach the Law, and how his teachings caused the marriage crisis.
- This early text was subsequently expanded by two sets of texts: Ezra's itinerary (Ezra 7.9, 28b; 8.15a, 21, 23, and 31-32) and Ezra's prayer (Ezra 9.1-3*, 5-7, 10-15*; 10.1a).
- This new version of EM is now combined with the early Ezra 5:1–6:15 as well as an early version of Ezra 1–4. At this point, the person responsible for this textual fusion (called the Rescript Editor) added the opening words in v. 7.1aα in order to join the EM to the preceding material in Ezra 1–6. He furthermore composed much of the material in Ezra 7 which introduces Ezra's first-person account. He is also the author of most of the first-person narrative in Ezra 8.24-29, 33-34.
- The text of Ezra and Nehemiah 8 subsequently underwent yet another redaction, whereby material which betrays an interest in the diaspora and in sacrifices was composed. These editors added material to Ezra 1–6 (Ezra 3.1-3, 6; 6.9-10, 16-17, 19-22), Ezra 7–10 (7.17-18; 8.35-36; 9.4; 10.3a, 6-9, 15a, 16) and Nehemiah 8 (8.13-17).
- At an even later point, smaller additions which reflect priestly and Levitical concerns were written to complement the by-now substantial body of text. These additions were placed strategically across Ezra 7–10 (7.7, 13, 24; 8.15b-20, 24b, 30, 33b, 10:5, 15b, 18), including the list of men of priestly and Levitical descent who had married unsuitable women (10.20-44) and scattered verses in Nehemiah 8 (7a, 11-13*). At the same time, the prayer in Nehemiah 9, as well as the list of people who had married women who were deemed to be foreign in Nehemiah 10, was written. Although Pakkala is open to the possibility that parts of the prayer may originally have existed independently elsewhere (p. 184), he nevertheless sees Nehemiah 9–10 as an example of the gradual growth (*Fortschreibung*) of the Ezra composition (Pakkala 2004: 210).
- Finally, the list of priestly families who left Babylon during the reign of Artaxerxes, found in Ezra 8.1-14, was added.

According to Pakkala, the notion of an EM, that is, an account written in the first person by a man named Ezra, is a literary fiction. Instead, the extant first-person account is the result of subsequent redactors (cf. Pakkala 2004: 55–6).

At this point, there is little in terms of a scholarly consensus on this matter (see the critique of Pakkala's model in Williamson 2007: 587). In my opinion, it is unlikely that we can determine the exact textual history of the text that we now call the EM. As to the historical value of the EM, I disagree with Pakkala's claim that it is fictional from beginning to end. At the same time, caution is required when using this text as the basis for historical reconstruction of the fifth century BCE. It is first and foremost a literary text with a clear theological agenda. As to the (possibly redactional) unity of Ezra 7–10 and Nehemiah 8, this theory convinces, as it pitches Nehemiah 8 as the (original and always intended) climax of Ezra's journey to Yehud.

Nehemiah 1–6, 13

The text of Nehemiah is also composite in nature. Again, readers encounter different types of material:

- Neh. 1–6: A first-person account which is narrated by Nehemiah.
- Neh. 7: A list of returning exiles (//Ezra 2, see above).
- Neh. 8: A third-person narrative featuring Ezra and Nehemiah together (see above).
- Neh. 9: A communal confession uttered in the first person plural.
- Neh. 10: A list of the people who sealed the agreement to follow the Torah.
- Neh. 11–12: Three distinct lists of people and places.
- Neh. 13: A first-person account of Nehemiah's dedication of the wall.

Two sections in Nehemiah are first-person narratives: Neh. 1–6 and Nehemiah 13. In view of their shared use of first-person speech, scholars speak of a NM which encompasses all/parts of the material in Neh. 1–6, 13. Two main models vis-à-vis the origin and structure of NM have been suggested, linking the question of genre of Neh. 1–6, 13 with the question of its composition history. According to the first model, NM originated as a type of *royal inscription*; according to the second model it originated as a *building report*. There are good arguments on both sides of the debate and there is no consensus in sight.

Nehemiah's memoir was modelled after royal inscriptions

Several scholars maintain that the NM was modelled in structure and style after ancient Near Eastern royal inscriptions: it introduces the protagonist, describes how he reached his position, lists his accomplishments and concludes with a prayer to preserve his memory. Parts of especially Neh. 5 and 13 adhere closely to this pattern, but traces of it can be found also in Neh. 2 and 6 (e.g. Blenkinsopp 1988: 46–7; Schottroff 1967: 218–22, 392–3). Most recently, Burt has offered a variant model along the same lines, suggesting that the original memoir consisted of Neh. 1.1–2.20; 3.33–7.3; 13.4-31. As to genre, Burt proposes that through consecutive and strategic additions, the text metamorphosed from being a court tale into being an official memoir, resulting in the final form of the text as a hybrid genre (Burt 2014).

Nehemiah's memoir originated as a building report

The alternative view is to see most of Neh. 1–6 as part of the original narrative, while treating select material as later additions. Williamson, for example, argues that the original narrative portrays Nehemiah's task as a short-term assignment related to the rebuilding of the wall (cf. Neh. 2.6). This narrative was written up as a report. It contained Neh. 1–4 (with the exception of the prayers in Neh. 1.4-11 and 3.36-37, as well as the list of builders in 3.1-32) and Neh. 5–6 (with the exception of Neh. 6.14). In contrast, the material in Neh. 5.14-19 and 13.4-31 which contains the positive 'remember' formula, as well as referring to the dedication of the wall, is secondary (Williamson 1985: xxv–xxviii). Modifying this theory, Reinmuth proposes that the original 'wall-building report' in Neh. 1–4 was a collaborate effort of the political leaders, priests and the people in Yehud, while the later revision (*Denkschrift*) which saw the additions of Neh. 5, 13 reveals social tension in the society between the upper (priests, political leaders) and the lower (people, Levites) classes (Reinmuth 2008: esp. 333–7). For a critique of this type of model, see Burt (Burt 2014: 34–45).

Two additional examples of redaction-critical schemes

There are also more elaborate schemes. In the present context, I shall showcase two different suggestions (by Wright and by Karrer) that each in its own way highlights the complexity of the Nehemiah material and its relation with the Ezra material. They further offer models for the reconstruction of the historical growth of Ezra-Nehemiah as a whole. Needless to say, they have both had their fair share of criticism, given the speculative aspects involved in all redaction-critical models (which is not meant as a critique, merely as a statement).

Wright's redaction-critical scheme

Falling into the same category as Williamson's and Reinmuth's schemes, Wright argues in favour of an original, very small, primary narrative about the wall (Neh. 1.1a, 11b; 2.1-6, 11, 15-18*; 3.38; and 6.15) (Wright 2004: 340). The remaining texts belong to one of six additional layers. These layers are not static sources that editors added to the core-text. Rather, they reflect a *process* whereby 'active readers' of the original building report read and gradually added their own reflections (Wright 2004: 330). An early redactional layer becomes a source that a subsequent reader can edit and interpret. The text that we have today is, according to Wright, the result of many such successive redactions.

Looking at the wider composition history of Ezra-Nehemiah, Wright detects a contradiction between those texts which portray the priesthood and the aristocracy as Nehemiah's opponents, and other texts which state that the High Priest initiated the reconstruction of the temple and that the aristocracy followed suit. This contradiction, in turn, is the key to the composition history of Ezra-Nehemiah (cf. Reinmuth). Wright argues for the primacy of the material in Neh. 1–6 (which grew gradually). The early form of Nehemiah's building report caused certain pro-priestly circles to respond and compose Ezra 1–6, and, in parallel, to write Ezra 7–8 to serve as a bridge between Ezra 1–6 and Nehemiah's account. At the last stage of development, Ezra 9–10 and Neh. 8–10 were inserted into the book. These texts again present Nehemiah in a more positive light than the preceding material in Ezra 1–8 (Wright 2004: 5–6).

1   The earliest textual layer formed a first-person account of Nehemiah's building of the wall. This very short core-text consisted of select material in Neh. 1–6 (Neh. 1.1a, 11b; 2.1-6, 11, 15-18*; 3.38; and 6.15).

2   The original first-person building account was expanded by material which offers more details such as a register of builders (3.1-32) and other material in Nehemiah 2 (2.9-18*). These additions served to change the focus of the account, away from the wall and on to the temple.

3   More material was written in order to show the positive results of the building project (Neh. 2.10, 19-20; 3.33-37; 4.1-17*; 5.16-18; 6.5-9, 16). This was done in part by describing the negative reaction to the project by Nehemiah's opponents.

4   Subsequently, material was composed which depicts Nehemiah as a governor and as the great builder of Jerusalem (Neh. 2.7, 9a; 5.14-15; 6.2-4).

5   New material was added which included some of Nehemiah's other activities besides rebuilding the wall. It was written in order to transform the existing account of the building of the wall into a wider account of the restoration of Yehud. The narrative in Neh. 1–6* was fleshed out (Neh. 1.1b-4; 5.1-13, 19; 6.10-14, 17-19) and, in parallel, the material in Neh. 13.4-30a, 31b was composed.

6   Following the attachment of the Nehemiah material to Ezra 1–6, additional material was added which relates primarily to the population and dedication of Jerusalem (Neh. 7.1-3; 11.1-2, 3-36; 12.27-47).

7   The final set of additions (Neh. 1.5-11a; 2:8; most of chs 7–10 and 12; 13.1-3, 30b-31a) was added at the same time as Ezra 7–10 was attached to Ezra 1–6. These additions together serve to balance the concentration on Torah study in Neh. 8–10 with the focus on the temple in Neh. 13.30b-31a.

Summing up, Wright argues that the Nehemiah's account gradually developed 'from a brief building report (or inscription) into an account of Judah's Restoration' (Wright 2004: 4).

Karrer's redaction-critical scheme

From a different perspective, Karrer has explored the difference in ideology regarding the idea of 'constitution' (*Verfassung*) between the 'Ezra source' and the 'Nehemiah source' and how the shifting focus of the various texts may shed light upon the gradual textual growth of Ezra-Nehemiah. She argues that the correct way of understanding these two works is to read them diachronically (i.e. in the order to their composition date) rather than synchronically (i.e. in the order in which they are presented in the extant Ezra-Nehemiah) (Karrer 2001).

Karrer postulates a three-stage development of Ezra-Nehemiah. The earliest material, found in the Nehemiah Source (Neh. 1.1–7.5; 12.27-43; 13.4-31), portrays Yehud as a society consisting both of returning exiles and people who had remained in the land. The defining issue for belonging within the community is thus not whether or not a person has returned from the exile but a matter of ethnicity. People who do not share this ethnic background (i.e. foreigners) must be excluded from the community. The power in this society rests with its sole leader Nehemiah, the governor (Karrer 2001: 149–61, 190–5).

The later material in the Ezra source (7.6, 28; 8.15-34; 9.1–10.44) is a conscious reaction to this model (Karrer 2004: 277–8). Karrer demonstrates that this source understands the community as consisting exclusively of returned exiles (cf. 10.8). Moreover, it preaches a more democratic model of government, where Ezra the scribe, the people's officials (cf. 9.1) and the people's assembly (cf. Ezra 10:1) together decide matters of importance (Karrer 2001: 240–3). Matters are religious rather than secular in nature, including who is part of the community and who is an outsider (i.e. a foreigner) (Karrer 2001: 267–71).

The Nehemiah Source and the Ezra Source are finally furnished with an editorial framework (Ezra 1–6; Neh. 7.6-72b; 11.21–12.26). The final form thus becomes a compromise between the positions of the two incorporated sources, with a society ruled by both a secular and a clerical leader, and which contains both secular and cultic sectors (Karrer 2001: 363–78 [conclusion]).

Nehemiah 8–10

In parallel with the aforementioned redaction-critical theories pertaining to Ezra 7–10 and Nehemiah 8, the material in Neh. 8–10 displays a certain thematic cohesion centred on the Law: the public reading of the Law (Nehemiah 8) and the repercussions of that reading (Neh. 9, 10). At the same time, Neh. 8–10 lacks the kind of uniformity that we would expect from a text which was authored by one person. In view of this diversity in terms of style and content, more than one scholar has postulated models for its gradual composition. We shall here look more carefully at the origin and function of the prayer in Nehemiah 9 and the list in Nehemiah 10.

The prayer in Nehemiah 9

A key concern in this discussion is the origin and function of the prayer in Nehemiah 9, following Ezra's reading of the Law in Nehemiah 8 (Newman 1999: 55–116; Duggan 2001: 157–233). In its present context, the prayer is presented as being uttered by the Levites (Neh. 9.5). It should be noted, however, that the prayer sits fairly loosely in its present context. The prayer refers to neither Ezra nor Nehemiah, and it lacks references to specific matters mentioned elsewhere in Ezra-Nehemiah. There is also little affinity between Nehemiah 9 on the one hand, and the prayers in Ezra 9 and Nehemiah 1 on the other. Finally, the ideology of Nehemiah 9 is distinct from the surrounding Ezra-Nehemiah (Tiemeyer 2008: 61). These discrepancies have given rise to the view that the author responsible for incorporating the prayer into the present context used an already existing prayer. Several scholars therefore argue that the prayer originated in early post-monarchic Yehud around 520 BCE or even earlier, that is, stemming from the indigenous Judahite community (Williamson 1988; Boda 1999: 189–95).

The alternative, less convincing in my view, is to see Nehemiah 9 as a text composed to fit its present place in Neh. 8–10. According to this view, Nehemiah 9 may never have had a historical setting (a *Sitz im Leben*) in the sense that it did not originate as a spontaneous prayer in a specific historical situation; it was instead composed to fit its current place in Nehemiah (*Sitz in der Literatur*) and later used liturgically as a prayer. Wright, for example, sees the whole chapter as a later, editorial addition, composed for its present literary setting (Wright 2004: 315–30; cf. Reinmuth 2008).

Nehemiah 10

In the final form of the text, the declaration of commitment by the community in Neh. 9.38–10.39 [Heb. 10.1-40] follows on from the prayer in the preceding Nehemiah 9. The list in Neh. 9.38–10.27 [Heb. 10.1-28], uttered in the first person plural, is headed by Nehemiah, the governor. The remaining material in vv. 28-39 [Heb. vv. 29-40] continues the first-person speech, where these people together with their families pledge to follow the Law: negatively, they will not intermarry and not trade on the Sabbath; positively, they will let the land rest every seventh year, support the temple sacrificial cult, and bring all first fruits to the temple. Although this speech can be read as the direct continuation of the prayer in Nehemiah 9, a compelling case can be made for reading it as an editorial subsection which in all likelihood is later than the material in Neh. 1–6 (13) (Blenkinsopp 1988: 311–12).

The lists in Nehemiah 11–12

The remaining material in Nehemiah, namely chs. 11 and 12, forms a bit of a mixed bag. As Japhet states, Neh. 11–12 constitutes a compilation of lists that are not integrated into the narrative but stand by themselves. Although these lists may have had a prehistory, in the sense that they existed as lists before being incorporated into Ezra-Nehemiah, it is unlikely that the present collection existed independently as a compilation (Japhet 1994: 195–6).

- The list in Neh. 11.1-24 consists of several smaller lists of people: (1) those who had settled in Jerusalem, including people from Yehud, from Benjamin, priests, and Levites (vv. 1-18); (2) other settlers, including gatekeepers and other types of temple servants (*nəṯînîm*) (vv. 19-21); and temple personnel (vv. 22-24) (Fulton 2015: 24).
- The following list in Neh. 11.25-36 enumerates the settlements in Yehud (vv. 25-30) and Benjamin (vv. 31-35), as well as a relatively obscure statement about Levitical settlements in the areas (Fulton 2015: 72).
- Finally, Neh. 12.1-26 lists the cultic officials who returned with Zerubbabel and Joshua, including the priestly leaders (vv. 1b-7), the Levitical leaders (vv. 8-9), the descendants of Joshua, the High Priest, until Jaddua (vv. 10-11), as well as a list of priestly and Levitical leaders who served in the temple when Joshua's son Jehoiakim was High Priest, and in the days of Nehemiah the governor and Ezra the scribe (vv. 12-26) (Fulton 2015: 126).

The earliest date of this material is the reign of Jaddua as High Priest, a reference which, following the genealogy, places us five generations later than Joshua who, according to the book of Haggai, was High Priest during the reign of Darius I (around 520 BCE). Following the writing of the Jewish historian Josephus (*Ant.* 11.304-320), this brings us to the last Persian king, Darius III (336–330 BCE), a contemporary of Alexander the Great.

Fulton has recently investigated these lists and reached the conclusion that they were likely composed in the early Hellenistic period (Fulton 2015: 199–200). She offers a multistage development of these lists. The Septuagint (LXX, i.e. the Greek translation of the Hebrew Bible) is based on an older Hebrew version, while a later, expanded version is preserved in the Masoretic Text (MT, the authoritative Hebrew and Aramaic text of the Hebrew Bible). Many of the additions in the later version concern temple institutions, where the cultic community as presented by the MT is significantly larger than the one in the earlier LXX. A third, even later, version of this material is preserved in 1 Chron. 9.10-18. According to Fulton, these additions aimed to show that the cultic presentations, important at a later date, also existed in the very small, fifth-century Jerusalem (Fulton 2015: 189–94). These lists further serve a literary purpose as they culminate the process, begun in Ezra 1–6, of rebuilding Jerusalem and of rededicating the temple. This association is facilitated through the reference to Joshua and Zerubbabel in Neh. 12.1 (Fulton 2015: 195–6).

Neh. 11–12 is also linked to the earlier list in Nehemiah 7, yet is unlikely to have been composed by the same author. Fulton argues that in an earlier version, Neh. 11–12 followed immediately on from Nehemiah 7. The material in Neh. 8–10 was inserted later. It is possible that the same editor responsible for adding Neh. 8–10 also made the above-mentioned changes to the lists in Neh. 11–12 (Fulton 2015: 198–9).

Who compiled the final form of Ezra-Nehemiah?

So far, we have looked at the individual texts that form Ezra-Nehemiah and explored the gradual development of this textual corpus until it reached the form that it has today. The fact that no consensus view exists can be seen as a direct result of the complex situation in Ezra-Nehemiah with various sources and changing authorial voices. We have also discussed the various authors of the different textual units, such as Ezra, Nehemiah, and a series of editors. What we have not touched upon, however, is the identity of the final editors. We shall here look at a range of approaches to the final form, with focus on two aspects. Who were the persons responsible for that final form and what message did they seek to convey? What were their professions, social positions and geographical setting and what did they seek to accomplish by compiling the text? Moreover, is Ezra-Nehemiah the work of a single group of people with a particular ideology (i.e. a school of thought), or can we detect different and changing ideologies in the various stages of textual growth?

A well-structured compilation organized by a single individual?

It is possible to argue that the message of the final text is identical with that of the individual pieces. In such cases, scholars tend to postulate that the editor is also the author of significant parts of the text. This approach does not necessarily mean that the individual texts are early and/or authentic. On the contrary, 'the author equals the editor approach' may imply that the editor composed many of the sections that other scholars treat as original documents.

Japhet's views illustrate 'the diachronic reading equals a synchronic reading' well. She takes the unusual and, to quote her own words, 'unpopular' approach that Ezra-Nehemiah is the work of a single person. She argues that as it is possible to read the material as the result of a single author, despite the complexity of the material, the reader is obliged to explain the composition of Ezra-Nehemiah in that way: 'as a book that was produced "all at once", by an author, according to a clear plan' (Japhet 1994: 200). This person organized the material and reshaped it to reflect two time periods: Ezra 1–6 depicts the time period between the first year of Cyrus's reign until the sixth year of Darius I's reign (twenty-six years); and Ezra 7–Nehemiah 13 depicts the time period from the seventh year of Artaxerxes I's reign to the thirty-third year of his reign (twenty-six years). These two time periods run parallel to one another, each featuring a diarchic leadership. In the first twenty-six years, we meet Zerubbabel the governor and Joshua the priest, and in the last twenty-six years we meet Nehemiah the governor and Ezra the priest/scribe (Japhet 1994: 208–10).

A well-structured compilation organized by a group of people?

Other scholars argue in favour of a specific group of people responsible for the traditions behind Ezra-Nehemiah. One key trend in contemporary scholarship is to assign a member/group of the clergy (e.g. a priest or Levite) to be the final editor. Williamson, for example, suggests that a group of priests was responsible for the compilation of Ezra-Nehemiah. The reason for the compilation was, so Williamson argues, that by 400 BCE, the memory of the two reformers Ezra and Nehemiah was beginning to fade away. By putting together Ezra 7–Nehemiah 13, the compiler aimed to reinvigorate the community by making the memory of the two men better known and to show that the physical restoration of Jerusalem and the community's separation from foreigners together constituted the prerequisites for the reception of the Law (Williamson 1985: xxxiv). Later, another editor added Ezra 1–6. By compiling the letters and lists, this latter editor sought: (1) to lend legitimacy to the works of Ezra and Nehemiah (Ezra 1–6 emphasized continuity between pre-exilic Judah and post-monarchic Yehud, and between the first and the second temple); and (2) to justify the rejection of the Samaritans and their offer to help with the building of the temple (Williamson 1985: xxxiv–xxxv).

In a more recent monograph, Min argues for Levitical editorship of Ezra-Nehemiah. He highlights that among all biblical texts from the post-monarchic period, Ezra-Nehemiah alone never assigns a minor role to the Levites. Furthermore, the emphasis of the unity of the people and the equal involvement of all the people in the building work point to a more democratic view of the community. These factors, according to Min, together suggest that a group of Levites, active in the late fifth century BCE, were responsible for the scroll. Moreover, given the positive view of Persian rule, it is possible that they received imperial backing (Min 2004).

Synchronic readings of Ezra-Nehemiah

This finally brings us to a synchronic reading of Ezra-Nehemiah (i.e. a reading which does not take the historical development of the text into account). Although the text of Ezra-Nehemiah is the result of extensive editorial work, ultimately what we have is the text before us. That text is meant to be read and that text has a message in its own right. The present sequence of texts is unlikely to be an accidental mishap; it is put together by an intelligent person, who arranged the various texts in a conscious manner in order to make a certain (theological) point (Childs 1979: 632–4).

A final-form approach to the text of Ezra-Nehemiah will ultimately contradict some of the insights of source- and redaction-critical scholars that we have discussed so far. As noted, many scholars turn to the aforementioned methods *because* they maintain that the final form *cannot* be read as a coherent narrative. Karrer, for example, argues that a linear reading of Ezra-Nehemiah does not make sense, insofar as it contains contradictions which cannot be mutually reconciled. A careful reading of the text reveals different views of what the society in Yehud is and ought to be (Karrer 2001: 107–24, 124–7). A final-form approach does not necessarily render a redaction-critical approach void, though, as it is possible to carry out the two investigations in parallel, as long as they are kept distinct. On the one hand, the authors of the individual texts wished to convey a certain message; on the other hand, the redactor responsible for the final form wished to convey another message.

It was Eskenazi who took upon herself to explore fully the literary aspects of Ezra-Nehemiah. Her leading question was: How does the final text *function as a story*? She maintains that Ezra-Nehemiah is a well-structured work which, in short, describes how the people of God built the temple in accordance with authoritative documents. The narrative itself falls into three parts:

1   Potentiality: Ezra 1.1-4
2   Process of Actualization: Ezra 1.5–Neh. 7.72
3   Success: Neh. 8.1–13.31.

Within this story, three key themes appear: the centrality of the people, the building of the temple and the notion that written documents are a source of authority (Eskenazi 1988: 175–6). Eskenazi further maintains that a single individual collected the sources and arranged them in their present order, with the purpose 'to exemplify the postexilic era as a time when Israel built the house of God in accordance with the divine work embodied in texts' (Eskenazi 1988: 185).

More than a decade later, Duggan produced a synchronic analysis of Neh. 7.72b–10.40, a text which is held together by its shared theme of covenant renewal. Rather than exploring matters of authorship and textual growth, Duggan focuses on the literary and theological features of the text before him. He asks, for example, how the shift in narrative voice functions within the final text of Neh. 7.72b–10.40, as well as within the wider context of Ezra-Nehemiah which also attests to such shifts (e.g. Ezra 7.27–9.15 *vs.* Ezra 10.1-44). He responds that, among other things, such shifts enable the people to speak directly to the audience of the book which, in turn, brings about a sense of immediacy (Duggan 2001: 291–2). Duggan further highlights how structural features such as the repetition of key vocabulary lend coherence and unity to the final form of Neh. 7.72b–10.40 (Duggan 2001: 293–5). Finally, turning to the issue of narrative progression, Duggan demonstrates that a synchronic reading of Neh. 7.72b–10.40 reveals the people's gradual acquaintance with and appropriation of the Torah (the Law). It passes through a gradually expanding circle of people, beginning with Ezra (Neh. 8.2-6), followed by the Levites (Neh. 8.7-8), the heads of the ancestral families (8.13), to end with the people as a whole (Neh. 9.3) (Duggan 2001: 295–7). Looking at a select detail, Duggan shows that when Neh. 7.72b–10.40 is being read synchronically, Neh. 8.9 (a verse which presents problems for a diachronic reading of Ezra-Nehemiah because Ezra and Nehemiah feature together) establishes a tie between the covenant renewal ceremony and Nehemiah's mission of rebuilding the wall (Duggan 2001: 115–16).

Dating

As to dating the material, it is likely that the process of the gradual compilation of Ezra-Nehemiah extended well into the Hellenistic period and possibly also into the Hasmonean period (cf. the MT of Neh. 11–12 above).

The relative dating of Ezra and Nehemiah

The text of Ezra-Nehemiah speaks of the three Persian monarchs–Cyrus, Darius and Artaxerxes. A notorious problem is, however, that the two latter names are shared by more than two people. In other words, there is a Darius I, II and III and there is an Artaxerxes I, II, III and IV. These ambiguities make it uncertain when *the texts themselves* envision the narrated events to have taken place.

There are, for example, three ways of dating Ezra's mission to Jerusalem. Ezra 7.1 states that Ezra travelled to Judah during the reign of Artaxerxes, and Ezra 7.8 states that he arrived in Judah in the seventh year of the reign of that king. To which monarch named Artaxerxes does the text refer? Depending on our decision, Ezra arrived in Judah either in 458 BCE (Artaxerxes I Longimanus, *r.* 465–424), or in 398 BCE (Artaxerxes II

Memnon, r. 404–358), or even in 351 BCE (Artaxerxes III Ochus, r. 358–338). Turning to Nehemiah, he travelled to Jerusalem the first time in the twentieth year of the reign of Artaxerxes (Neh. 2.1) and stayed there for twelve years, that is, the thirty-second year of the reign of Artaxerxes (Neh. 5.14), during which time he built the city wall. Nehemiah subsequently returned to Jerusalem (Neh. 13.6-7) at which time he dealt with marriages between women from Ashdod, Ammon, and Moab and Jewish men (Neh. 13.23-30). Is this the same Artaxerxes, or is it a different one?

A key to this conundrum lies in the reference to the High Priest Jaddua, the great-great-grandson of Joshua, in Neh. 12.10-11, 22. According to this reference, Jaddua lived during the reign of Darius (v. 22). It cannot be Darius I as he lived and reigned in the sixth century BCE, at the time of the building of the temple (cf. Ezra 4.5), that is, at the time of Jaddua's great-great-grandfather. This leaves us with Darius II Ochus (r. 423–405 BCE) or the last king of the Persian Empire, Darius III Codomannus (r. 336–330 BCE).

According to Josephus (*Ant.* xi, vii, 2), the biblical account in Nehemiah 12 refers to the last king of Persia, thus Darius must be identified with Darius III. Jaddua would then have seen the end of the Persian Empire and lived through the conquest of Alexander the Great. According to this identification, Ezra-Nehemiah cannot have been compiled earlier than the Hellenistic period. There are, however, problems with this view. First, this would make the list of priests in Nehemiah 12 very long. Secondly, there is also no indication in Nehemiah 12 that the Persian Empire has come to an end (Min 2004: 33-4).

Alternatively, if we maintain that Ezra arrived during the reign of Artaxerxes I and that Jaddua was active during the reign of Darius II, we may have a date of compilation of Ezra-Nehemiah in the late fifth century BCE (Min 2004: 34-5).

This conundrum has impact upon the relative chronology of Ezra and Nehemiah: who arrived in Yehud first? When we read Ezra-Nehemiah sequentially, following the chronology that is implied by the canonical presentation of Ezra-Nehemiah, Ezra precedes Nehemiah.

There are, however, many scholars who argue for the opposite order. Rothenbusch, for example, maintains that Nehemiah served as governor in Yehud in the middle of the fifth century BCE, that is, during the reign of Artaxerxes I (465–424 BCE). In contrast, Ezra arrived in Jerusalem only in the beginning of the fourth century, that is, during the reign of Artaxerxes II (405–359 BCE). Ezra's arrival in Yehud coincided with Persia's loss of military control over Egypt (Rothenbusch 2012: 284–326; cf. Fried 2015: 142–3, 289–90, 293–4).

The references in Ezra 9.9bβ to the Hebrew word gāḏêr is one key reason for postulating Nehemiah's arrival prior to Ezra's arrival. If the word gāḏêr means 'wall', then it is reasonable to assume that Ezra is writing about a time which post-dates Nehemiah's building of the city wall. The fact that the term gāḏêr does not normally denote a city wall (the normal Hebrew word for 'city wall' is ḥōmāh), however, makes the situation more complicated. Elsewhere in the Hebrew Bible, the word gāḏêr is used metaphorically (e.g. Ps. 80.12). Further, the reference to Judah alongside Jerusalem suggests that the text refers to something different than a city wall. For these reasons, it is possible to translate Ezra 9.9bβ as 'to provide a secure place in Judah and Jerusalem' (Williamson 1985: 59–62; Min 2004: 32–3).

Bibliography of key studies

Burt, Sean. *The Courtier and the Governor: Transformations of Genre in the Nehemiah Memoir* (JAJS, 17; Göttingen: Vandenhoeck & Ruprecht, 2014).

Duggan, Michael W. *The Covenant Renewal in Ezra-Nehemiah, (Neh 7:72b-10:40): An Exegetical, Literary, and Theological Study* (SBLDS, 164; Atlanta, GA: SBL, 2001).

Eskenazi, Tamara Cohn. *In an Age of Prose: A Literary Approach to Ezra-Nehemiah* (SBLMS, 36: Atlanta, GA: Scholars Press, 1988).

Fried, Lisbeth S. (ed.), *Was 1 Esdras First? An Investigation into the Priority and Nature of 1 Esdras* (Ancient Israel and Its Literature, 7; Atlanta, GA: SBL, 2011).

Fulton, Deirdre N. *Reconsidering Nehemiah's Judah* (FAT, II/80; Tübingen: Mohr Siebeck, 2015).

Grabbe, Lester L. 'The "Persian Documents" in the Book of Ezra: Are They Authentic?' in Oded Lipschits and Manfred Oeming (eds), *Judah and the Judeans in the Persian Period* (Winona Lake, IN: Eisenbrauns, 2006), pp. 531–70.

Japhet, Sara. 'The Supposed Common Authorship of Chronicles and Ezra-Nehemiah Investigated Anew', *VT* 18 (1968), pp. 330–71.

Karrer, Christiane. *Ringen um die Verfassung Judas: Eine Studie zu den theologisch-politischen Vorstellungen im Esra-Nehemia-Buch* (BZAW, 308; Berlin: de Gruyter, 2001).

Min, Kyung-jin. *The Levitical Authorship of Ezra-Nehemiah* (JSOTS, 409; London: T & T Clark International, 2004).

Pakkala, Juha. *Ezra the Scribe: The Development of Ezra 7–10 and Nehemiah 8* (BZAW, 347; Berlin; de Gruyter, 2004).

Redditt, Paul L. 'The Dependence of Ezra-Nehemiah on 1 and 2 Chronicles', in Mark H. Boda and Paul L. Redditt (eds), *Unity and Disunity in Ezra-Nehemiah: Redaction, Rhetoric, and Reader* (HBM, 17; Sheffield: Sheffield Phoenix Press, 2008), pp. 216–40.

Rothenbusch, Ralf. '… *Abgesondert zur Tora Gottes hin*': *Ethnische und religiöse Identitäten im Ezra/Nehemiabuch* (Herders biblische Studien, 70; Freiburg: Herder, 2012).

Throntveit, Mark A. 'Linguistic Analysis and the Question of Authorship in Chronicles, Ezra and Nehemiah', *VT* 32 (1982), pp. 201–16.

Williamson, H. G. M. *Israel in the Books of Chronicles* (Cambridge: Cambridge University Press, 1977).

Wright, Jacob L. *Rebuilding Identity: The Nehemiah-memoir and its Earliest Readers* (BZAW, 372; Berlin; de Gruyter, 2004).

3

The Situation in Post-Monarchic Yehud

Even if Ezra-Nehemiah ultimately is a literary creation which strives towards portraying a specific literary and theological situation, we should not forget that it was: (1) written in; and (2) set in specific historical circumstances. The present chapter therefore sets out to explore the situation in post-monarchic Yehud. In short, what was it like to live there in the fifth century BCE? This chapter further discusses the role of Yehud within the larger Persian Empire. What was the relationship between Yehud and its imperial overlord? How much influence did the local community in Yehud have, when it came to deciding their policy and their religious customs? This discussion touches upon two important issues, namely, Ezra's role in the compilation of the Torah (Pentateuch) and Nehemiah's role in the framing of the overarching imperial policy of defence against Egypt.

Yehud, a society in ruins

How many people lived in Yehud at the time of Ezra and Nehemiah? In order to answer that question, we have to revisit two interrelated questions. When were the different parts of Ezra-Nehemiah written, and do the individual texts reflect the time of the narrated events or the time of their composition? Given the relatively wide scope of uncertainty, we shall look in general at the entire Persian period, with focus on the fifth and the fourth century BCE.

Jerusalem and Judah were destroyed in 586 BCE by the Neo-Babylonian armies. The available archaeological data from the sixth century suggest that nearly all settlements were either destroyed or abandoned at this time. Furthermore, this catastrophic event decimated the population of Judah and, as Faust demonstrates, the population continued to decrease in the years following the destruction. Faust assesses the lowest demographic point to reach no higher than 10 per cent of the pre-exilic population (Late Iron Age). The reasons for this immense demographic decline are many. Faust suggests some frightful reasons for the death toll. Given no effective medicines, combined with the lack of sterile conditions, many people in Jerusalem would have died from their wounds. Others would have died from famine and epidemics both during and after the siege. We also need to remember the executions after the fall of the city, combined with people fleeing the area. Thus, even if a relatively low percentage of the overall population of pre-exilic Judah were exiled to Babylon, not many of those left behind would have survived. As a result, the population of post-war Judah would have been very low indeed (Faust 2012: 140–3).

Faust speculates on what life might have been like in the second half of the sixth century, that is, the society to which the first exiles would have returned. There would have been a population, reaching mere thousands, who would have been living scattered throughout the land, some amid the ruined cities and some in 'islands of settlements' throughout the devastated countryside. They would have subsisted on simple agriculture, but they would have had no surplus to use for trade. Large kinship groups would not have survived, but there might have been some kind of loose economic and social structure in place. A fair degree of social mobility would have existed, which might have enabled individuals to rise above their original status to leadership positions (Faust 2012: 233–42).

The question is, then, how quickly the post-monarchic Judahite society would have regained the wealth and population that they lost in 586 BCE.

There are different views on this question and we shall here take both textual and archaeological evidence into account. Again, following Faust, it took centuries for the area to recover and to reach the pre-586 BCE demographic level. It is therefore important not to overestimate the population in Persian period Yehud. It is likely that the population remained very small throughout the entire era, and that any real recovery took place only in the Hellenistic period (Faust 2012: 137–9, 172–3). Faust classifies Yehud as a 'post-collapse society', which is characterized by simple economy, political fragmentation, few monumental buildings, few people with specialized skills and lack of trade. 'Judah during the entire Persian period should therefore still be viewed as a post-collapse society' (Faust 2012: 168–73).

Yehud, a very small part of the Persian Empire

We have just seen that Yehud did not have a large population. Nor did it cover an impressive geographical area. On the contrary, its size was very small. We are thus dealing with a small, sparely populated, predominantly rural, insignificant part of the Persian Empire. Anyone reading Ezra-Nehemiah will notice that the Persian Empire is depicted in very positive terms. The Persian monarch was very friendly towards the Israelites in exile, he supported the returnees financially, and he supported the individual missions of Ezra (Ezra 7) and Nehemiah (Nehemiah 1) (Becking 1999: 256–75). What is the reason for this positive portrayal, and how well does it agree with the historical circumstances?

The organization of the Persian Empire

Cyrus conquered Babylon in 539 BCE. He inherited a large area which covered all of Mesopotamia (Babylonia), as well as the area called Beyond the River (*Ebar Nahara*/Trans-Euphrates). Initially, this vast area formed one administrative unit, called 'satrapy'. In addition, after Persia's conquest of Egypt, this region came to form an additional satrapy. Subsequently, during the reign of Darius I (522/521–486 BCE), the satrapy of Babylonia and Beyond the River was subdivided, with the latter forming a subunit within Babylonia. Even later, during the reign of Darius I's successor Xerxes, the satrapy of Beyond the River was separated from Babylonia and given equal status. At this point, Beyond the River was the fifth satrapy, Egypt was the sixth satrapy, and Babylon was the ninth satrapy. There were in total twenty satrapies. This situation continued until the end of the Persian period (Lipschits 2006: 24–5).

The power of Jerusalem

Most readers tend to assume that Jerusalem was the capital of Yehud. This is a reasonable assumption, given that the activities of Ezra and Nehemiah are totally centred on Jerusalem. The ruined temple was being rebuilt and the ruined city walls were being restored. Does this picture correspond to historical reality, though, insofar as political power goes? Was Jerusalem the civic centre or was its influence restricted to the cultic sphere?

It is reasonably clear that Jerusalem was not an urban centre in the Persian period. Speaking about the whole area that used to constitute the Northern and the Southern Kingdoms of Israel and Judah, Lipschits maintains that Samaria was the main town throughout the early post-monarchic period, as evidenced by archaeology (Lipschits 2006: 30–1). This, however, does not automatically mean that Yehud formed a small part of the province of Samaria, as was often argued by earlier scholars. Rather, as suggested by Lipschits and others, it is more likely that Yehud formed a small but distinct province throughout the entire Persian period (Lipschits 2006: 34–5).

In the beginning of the post-monarchic era, Jerusalem was probably not the administrative centre of Yehud. As indicated by the material in Jer. 40–44, the Neo-Babylonian officials appointed Gedaliah as governor and placed him in Mizpah, a settlement north of Jerusalem. Nothing suggests that Mizpah ceased to be the administrative centre following the assassination of Gedaliah (Jer. 41.1-8). Further, even though the temple was rebuilt already around 515 BCE and thus functioned as a cultic centre for the people of Yehud, it is possible that the ruined city wall prevented Jerusalem from serving as the regional capital (Lipschits 2006: 35).

Bedford has argued that the temple in Jerusalem does not seem to have been the administrative centre of the city. Instead, based on an examination of coins and stamps, the centre was located at the nearby area of Ramat Rachel. Bedford continues by arguing that the Persian Empire was not interested in supporting local cults, as scholars have often assumed. The main interest in the cult was that it served the purpose of covering the cost of their administration. They did not *fund* the cult; they *taxed* the cult (Bedford 2015: 341). Bedford further discusses the relative political weakness of the priesthood. On the basis of the material in Nehemiah and corroborated by that in the Haggai-Malachi corpus, the political power of the priesthood in post-monarchic Yehud was limited to affairs which directly referred to the temple and its cult. The governor had markedly more power and the priests deferred to him (Bedford 2015: 342–6).

The textual evidence of Nehemiah suggests that a change took place in the middle of the fifth century BCE. Lipschits postulates a move of the administration from Mizpah to Jerusalem at this time, as outlined in the NM and as supported by the scant archaeological remains of a city wall from this time period (Lipschits 2006: 35–40). The question is what triggered this change and what made Persia allow or support or even initiate the restoration of the wall around Jerusalem.

Persia and Nehemiah's mission: The building of Jerusalem's city wall

According to Neh. 1–2, Nehemiah's main reason for wishing to go to Jerusalem was the ruined state of the city wall around it. The rebuilding of the wall is subsequently also the main topic of the Nehemiah Memoir (Neh. 1–4, 6–7, 12.27-43). According to the biblical account, the Persian monarch encouraged and supported the building project. The question here is 'why'. What was in it for Persia?

One key theory, advocated by Hoglund, is that the fortification of Jerusalem was part of a wider plan in the fifth century BCE to tighten the control of the Levant and to create a military buffer against Egypt. Hoglund argues his case through an investigation of predominantly Greek texts which speak of the so-called Egyptian Revolt in the middle of the fifth century BCE that caused significant unrest throughout the eastern Mediterranean coast. In response to this rebellion, the Persian Empire sought to strengthen its control over the Levant. One way was to erect imperial garrisons in strategic places, among them being Yehud and the coastal plain. According to Hoglund, Ezra's and Nehemiah's missions to Yehud should be seen as part of this strategy, namely, to create a web of economic and social relationships which tied the periphery of the Empire closer to its centre. In particular, Nehemiah's task to erect the city walls of Jerusalem, combined with his social and economic reforms, aimed to alter the relationship between the central imperial powers and the outlying territory of Yehud. In the case of Ezra, the focal point was more on legal reform. Taken together, the Persian Empire sought 'to compel loyalty to the imperial system by tying the community's self-interest to the goals of the empire' (Hoglund 1992).

It should, however, be pointed out that there is little in terms of direct evidence for Hoglund's theory. No Persian documents refer to Yehud as an important location near the Egyptian border, despite the fact that several Persian documents mention Egypt and bring up the question of military strategy. It further needs to be noted that there is no support for this theory within the biblical material itself. Nehemiah (rather than the king) initiated his journey to Jerusalem because the city was in ruins (and not for any military reason). Further, the walls were used to keep certain people in Yehud from entering into the city (and not in order to protect the borders) (Grabbe 2001: 110).

In addition, it is often easy for biblical scholars to overestimate the significance of little Yehud in the wider imperial scheme of things. In short, why would a fortified Jerusalem, situated in the hill country, be of strategic military significance to Persia in its conflict with Egypt? There would be few compelling reasons why anyone travelling between Persia and Egypt would journey via Jerusalem rather than along the Mediterranean coast (Lipschits 2006: 37–8).

Other scholars relate the reasons for Jerusalem's rise to administrative significance to factors internal to Yehud. Schaper, for example, argues that the temple in Jerusalem gradually came to serve not only as a cultic centre but also as an administrative centre in charge of gathering taxes and carrying out other fiscal tasks on behalf of the Persian central government (Schaper 1995; Lipschits 2006: 38–9). The gradual change came to serve as the impetus for allowing the city walls of Jerusalem to be fortified. To cite Lipschits, the Persian authorities agreed to (Nehemiah's) requests 'when they realized that, besides its status as the ideological and literary center, Jerusalem had already become the fiscal center of the province' (Lipschits 2006: 40).

Persia and Ezra's mission

Ezra 7 introduces us to the character of Ezra. Verse 6 describes him as a 'scribe skilled in the Law of Moses' and declares that the king 'had granted him everything he asked'. Ezra accordingly journeys to Jerusalem, bringing with him a letter from the Persian king, Artaxerxes, which assigns to him a set of tasks and gives him the authority necessary to carry them out. Verse 14 informs us that Ezra is supposed to 'inquire about Judah and Jerusalem with respect to the Law of your God'. He is given money to buy sacrificial animals (vv. 15-17) and a carte blanche to 'do with the rest of the money in accordance with the will of your God' (v. 18). The same letter further declares that the temple personnel in Jerusalem are to be exempt from paying tax (v. 24). Finally, v. 25 gives Ezra another major task, namely, 'to appoint magistrates and judges to administer justice to all the people of "Beyond the River" who know the laws of your God'. This task has a sub-task, that is, to teach those that do not know these laws. Verse 26 offers another specification: anyone who does not obey 'the Law of [his] God and the law of the King' (v. 26) will be punished.

As already noted in ch. 1, this is a fictional account insofar as it is part of the overall literary narrative about Ezra's accomplishments. This fictional quality, however, does not in itself preclude the possibility that it provides historically accurate descriptions of historical event and, as such, can teach us about the situation in Yehud in the fifth century BCE. As Blenkinsopp argues, the final statement in Ezra 7.26 appears to indicate that the Persian king had the final say and that Ezra was authorized to enforce Persian law (Blenkinsopp 2001: 55–6).

Speaking only about the royal letter, it is difficult to determine whether it is a genuine document or not. As Grabbe highlights, it contains linguistic features which reflect a type of Aramaic that was written in post-Achaemenid texts (i.e. texts composed after 330 BCE). This fact alone suggests that the letter was composed after the Persian era. Therefore, according to Grabbe, at most we can say that a genuine Persian decree might possibly lie behind the present text (Grabbe 2001: 92–4).

What exactly was Ezra appointed to do? As Fried highlights, the letter is phrased in such a way as to make clear that the main task for which Artaxerxes commissioned Ezra is really to appoint judges in Beyond the River so that they in turn can administer justice upon two subsets of people: those who know the laws of Ezra's God and those who do not know these laws. Fried argues that according to the Persian judicial system, the local governors would have appointed the provincial judges (such as local judges in Yehud). In contrast, only the king or his agents would have appointed judges at a satrapal level. Thus, Ezra 7 is portraying Ezra as a royal agent whose task is to appoint royal judges on a satrapal level (Fried 2001: 65–7). Fried continues to argue, supported by her investigation of the Egyptian and Mesopotamian textual evidence, that the king/his agents based their rulings on their own understanding of the law. There is no evidence of local participation in the decision-making (Fried 2001: 67–72). Not only that, there is very little evidence that law-codes in the ancient world served as a book of legal rulings and that judges ever consulted them. Rather, the law-codes constituted 'scientific description[s] of justice as a political ideal'. Practical justice was carried out in line with each society's 'own socially constructed ideas of fairness and right'. Returning to Ezra, his task was thus to appoint judges who would make judicial decisions in line with the Persian sense of justice (rather than in accordance with any local book of laws). It follows that Ezra's task should not be confused with the formation of the Pentateuch (cf. below) (Fried 2001: 72–84). In support of her claim, Fried argues that Nehemiah's decreed punishments were often in line with Persian rulings (e.g. the pulling of beards in Neh. 13.23-25), yet his rulings were probably also based on his own sense of justice (e.g. Neh. 13.15-22). His enforcement of the Sabbath coincided with the laws pertaining to the Sabbath in the Pentateuch, yet the Pentateuch was not the *source* of his authority (Fried 2001: 84–8). This interpretation raises a query about the statement 'the law of your God' in Ezra 7.25. If Fried's interpretation is correct, the reference to those who know 'the laws of Your God' simply becomes a way of identifying Jews.

Alternatively, this phrase can be read as evidence for the Persian authorization of this Law (cf. Frei below). According to this latter line of thinking, Artaxerxes is commissioning Ezra to write/compile the Pentateuch which, in turn, will be legally binding, due to the Persian seal of approval, to the Jews living in the satrapy of Beyond the River. The issue becomes more complicated when seeking to identify the next group of people, namely, those 'who do not know' the laws. Who are they: Jews ignorant of the Law or non-Jews?

Knoppers looks at this issue from a slightly different angle, as he asks to what degree 'the law of your God' and 'the law of the King' can be equated. More exactly, he deliberates whether imperial law and local (religious) law were conceived to be distinct, complementary, related or identical. The text of Ezra seems to suggest some kind of division; the question is whether such a division has historical value (Knoppers 2001: 122–3). In search of the answer, Knoppers explores two texts from Chronicles (assumed also to have been written in the Persian period) (1 Chron. 23.1–27.34, dealing with David's establishment of an administrative system to support Solomon in his future reign, and 2 Chron. 17.9–19.11, Jehoshaphat's establishment of a legal system). In view of these two narratives, Knoppers postulates that Persian

Jewish authors demarcated between the cultic and the royal legal realms (Knoppers 2001: 123–9).

Turning to the question of local authority, Knoppers considers it likely that the local leaders had considerable autonomy when it came to determining sacred laws. The Achaemenid central government was content to allow local communities a fair amount of freedom to observe their own customs and religious traditions. Any kind of highly centralized Persian policy in this respect would have been very costly and time-consuming. This approach served the central government well, as it tended to generate more revenue from the provinces and greater allegiance on the part of the local appointees (Knoppers 2001: 129–31, 134). To illustrate his point, Knoppers discusses Nehemiah's regulations of the temple cult (Nehemiah 13) and the commitments of the community towards it (Nehemiah 10). He suggests that these measures were unlikely to be the result of an imperial decree; they are rather Nehemiah's own (local) interpretation of the Davidic procedure of establishing offices for the Levitical singer, with which the central imperial powers had no wish to be concerned (Knoppers 2001: 131–3).

Persia and the temple

The textual evidence for Persian involvement in the building of the temple in Jerusalem in the fifth century BCE can be found in several places in Ezra-Nehemiah. In Ezra 7.16-20, for example, the Persian monarch, Artaxerxes, authorizes Ezra to bring funds from the royal treasury to equip the temple and to buy animals for sacrifice (i.e. all that is needed for a functioning cult). Statements like these raise a series of questions pertaining to the role of the Persian Empire in the rebuilding of the temple. Did the Persians fund the building project? If they did, what did they expect to receive in return? Moreover, what was Persia's role in the running of the temple once it had been rebuilt? Did they have the overall control of its cultic practices and did they seek to influence its organization? In response, scholarly views have tended to fall into one of three (partly overlapping) categories.

One theory is that the central Persian administration exercised a strict control over the various part of the Empire in order to ensure that taxes and resources found their way from the outskirts of the Empire to its heartland. As a result, the local governing bodies (such as the native elite) had little control over their customs and resources. Some of the main advocates among biblical scholars of this theory are Cataldo and Fried.

Cataldo makes a solid case for fairly heavy-handed Persian control over its provinces. Persia's tolerance of local customs and cults should not be confused with local autonomy. Regional religious leaders had certain power over cultic issues, but only as long as they remained loyal to the Empire. Likewise, local temples were allowed to be restored but, along with their cultic function, they were organs of the Persian fiscal administration. Finally, all local leaders were appointed by the imperial government and could easily be removed (Cataldo 2009: 33–66).

Fried surveys a wide range of primary texts (from Babylon, Egypt, and Asia Minor) dated to the Persian period in Babylon. She notes that these texts support the notion of imperial control over temples (rather than imperial authorization or self-rule, cf. above) (Fried 2004: 8–155). Assuming that the situation in Yehud would be comparable, she argues that the evidence in Ezra-Nehemiah, as well as in Haggai, Zech. 1–8 and Isa. 56–66, points in the same direction. Yehud had no assemblies and no Jewish lay bodies to advise the governor. There is also no evidence of any type of vehicle for local control. Local leaders held little real power. Although the people connected with the temple in Jerusalem construed their identity around the temple, power rested in the hand of Persia (Fried 2004: 156–233).

A second theory advocates the imperial authorization of local customs (see especially Frei below). According to this line of thinking, the Empire encouraged the local community to keep its customs and cultic practices.

The third way of looking at the situation is to argue that the Persian Empire was not very interested in local cultic practices and therefore granted the local rulers a fair degree of self-governance. As long as the taxes kept coming in as they should, the details as to how they were gathered were left to the local governor.

Dandamayev argues that the various groups of conquered people in the Persian Empire lived in a fairly moderate ideological climate. In comparison to later time periods, they encountered less pressure of official ideology and religious ideas. Dandamayev further maintains that the central government seldom interfered with local social and economic structures and existing traditions. In fact, the imperial administration was not overly involved in the intellectual life of the subjected peoples. The legal and cultic development in the conquered areas of, for example, Egypt, Babylonia, and Yehud, was not due to any central Persian pressure but instead a result of internal factors. 'The Persian authorities were only concerned with creating a stable administration and establishing an efficient system for collecting royal taxes' (Dandamayev 1999). Jigoulov also argues for a managed autonomy as an administrative system. His views are based on an investigation of the Phoenician city states which were allowed to run their affairs relatively unhindered. In Jigoulov view, this situation may illustrate how the Persian kings administered also other areas. They assigned autonomy to the individual territories and allowed them to manage their own affairs free of direct oversight (Jigoulov 2009: 138–51).

In this discussion, it is important to distinguish between the rich coastal areas, of which the Phoenician city states would be examples, and the much poorer hill country (of Yehud). As argued by Lipschits, the Persians had no interest in encouraging and developing urban centres in the hill country. They served best as agricultural areas and, as such, easily controllable areas (Lipschits 2006: 26–9).

Briant also advocates a certain internal autonomy. Speaking of the administration of tribute, Briant argues that a local leader was put in charge of each ethnic group initially. These native leaders were then gradually replaced by Persian officials. At the same time, local structures were often maintained and the Persians recognized the authority of local leaders. So, the (Persian) satrap oversaw the ruler within each district, yet each local ruler was responsible for bringing his portion of tribute to that satrap. This spared the satrap from getting involved in local disputes. Briant concludes that the installation of an 'imperial administrative machine' does not destroy local customs but instead depends upon them (Briant 2002: 410–11, 471). In the particular case of Egypt, Briant argues that all the high-ranking officials were Persians who, in turn, had Egyptians in their service. There was a mutual interchange of traditions. While the Persian officials adopted some of the ways of Egypt, in parallel the Egyptian elite tried to emulate Persian practices (Briant 2002: 481–3). Turning to Yehud, the biblical portrayal in Ezra-Nehemiah seems to point towards internal autonomy, while at the same time also exhibits submission to Persia in terms of paying tribute (Briant 2002: 487–8).

Persia and the Torah

The concept of the Torah plays a major role in Ezra-Nehemiah. This fact has raised a number of issues. What is the extent of the Torah at this time (i.e. what texts in the current Pentateuch were included in this collection)? How should the idea of 'Torah' in Ezra-Nehemiah be understood (by the authors of Ezra-Nehemiah/by the people in Yehud)? What was the role of the Persian Empire in the creation and authorization of the Torah? To what extent did they form the impetus for the codification of the Jewish Law and to what extent did they organize and even supervise this endeavour? Many theories abound and we shall explore the textual support of some of the more influential ideas.

Beginning with the biblical accounts, the statement in Ezra 7 that Artaxerxes authorized Ezra's Law-book forms the textual basis on which the idea of an imperial authorization of the Torah is based. First of all, Ezra 7.6 introduces us to Ezra and describes him as a 'scribe skilled in the Law of Moses'. Furthermore, Ezra 7.14 states that Ezra carries with him a letter from the Persian king which claims that he is authorized, among other things, 'to inquire about Judah and Jerusalem with respect to the Law of your God'. The same letter further declares that Ezra will teach the people 'the laws of [his] God' (Ezra 7.25), and that anyone who does not obey 'the Law of [his] God and the law of the King' (Ezra 7.26) will be punished.

There is possibly support for Persia's involvement in Yehud's affairs in Nehemiah's statement in Neh. 13.30-31 that he assigned duties to the priests and Levites. This claim is informed in part by the statement in Neh. 11.23 about the singers in the temple being 'under the king's order' and in Neh. 11.24 that Pethahiah was 'the king's hand in all affairs relating to the people'. As Frei argues, the 'king' here is the Persian ruler. Thus, Pethahiah was his agent or advisor (Frei 2001: 13–14; cf. Blenkinsopp 2001: 52–3). Lastly, the fictional account in the book of Esther may shed inadvertent light upon Persian involvement in Jewish affairs, as it speaks of Mordechai who, in his role as grand vizier, establishing the celebration of *Purim* (Esth. 9.20-28) and how this decree was endorsed by Queen Esther and subsequently confirmed (Esth. 9.29-32). Thus, according to the author of Esther, a royal endorsement lends credence to a religious Jewish celebration (Frei 2001: 16–17).

Turning to extra-biblical accounts, we have a wide array of texts which uphold the idea that Persia was involved in and supported the creation of local legislation. There is, for example, Egyptian evidence to suggest that Darius I supported the codification of laws governing Egypt (Frei 2001: 9–10). Speaking more specifically about the Jewish community in Elephantine, Egypt, the so-called Passover Letter speaks of Darius I's involvement in the structure of the Passover celebration (Frei 2001: 15–16). Beyond the ancient Near East, there is also evidence of imperial engagement in local legal affairs from various places in Asia Minor (Greece, Lycia) (Frei 2001: 18–21). There are also other cases from Egypt (e.g. the attempts of the

Egyptian official Udjahorresnet to make the Persian emperor acknowledge and respect Egyptian customs and practices, and a command of Darius I which seems to have a bearing on the selection of priests in Elephantine) and from Asia Minor which involve Persian officials, yet it is not clear whether these same officials really authorized the proceedings (Frei 2001: 22–9).

Our understanding of Ezra's role *versus* the imperial role is influenced by our understanding of the amount of self-rule that Yehud had. What were the limits of the local autonomy of a province or sub-province in sixth-century Persia? In general, in order to consolidate their rule over a given conquered territory, the Persian ruling classes handed over much of the local administrative responsibilities to the locals who, in turn, were responsible to the central administration. While it was important for the central authority to oversee the local rulers, it was also important to protect local customs and to respect local regulations (Frei 2001: 6–7).

Scholars differ from one another in their understanding of these statements. Many scholars see the laws in the Pentateuch as the Jewish example of local regulations. The Persian Empire needed a document which outlined the local customs and laws prevalent in Yehud and thus commissioned and authorized the formation and codification of the Pentateuch. This decree prompted different groups in Yehud to gather together their distinct traditions. In particular, it caused the priests to compile the Priestly Source and it caused the elders to compile what later came to be the book of Deuteronomy. The strength of this theory is that it explains satisfactorily why there are contradictions and also doublets in the Pentateuch: the result is not only a compilation but also a *compromise*, commissioned by the Persian authorities (see further Ska 2001: 162–3).

The prime advocate of this view is Frei. On the basis of the textual evidence cited above, Frei argues that the notion of imperial authorization fits with Achaemenid administrative practices. He further maintains that it was relatively easy for subordinates to reach the Persian government with a request (cf. Nehemiah). He postulates a certain interaction and cooperation between the local and the imperial realm, as the king was able to impose his will upon a local community yet the local community also had the possibility to turn local policy into imperial policy (Frei 2001: 35, 39–40).

Other scholars are more hesitant in the matter, pointing out various potential problems with Frei's assertions. Bedford re-examines the claim that Darius I was the first to 'codify' Egyptian law. This claim is based on a series of primary sources, among them the list of Egyptian law-givers in Diodorus's writings (a classic author writing in Greek). According to Bedford, the notion of a 'lawgiver' is alien to Egyptian way of thinking. The extant Greek list is possibly an attempt by Diodorus to 'Hellenize' an Egyptian institution in order to enable his own Greek audience to understand the concept, but leaving the matter unrecognizable to a native Egyptian. Turning to Egyptian legal writing, Bedford argues that the two centuries prior to the Persian conquest saw a significant understanding and development of Egypt's legal tradition. The time between 711 and 525 BCE were 'characterized by a diligent search in libraries for old texts and a resuscitation of obsolete phraseology and formulas', which resulted in the copying and publication of new legal texts and new legal models vis-à-vis property law, contract law and tax law. This was already in place when Darius I entered the Egyptian scene. What could he do but to 'authorize' it? In fact, it is likely that Darius I's endeavour was more of a 'translation' of the already existing Egyptian legal material into Aramaic in order to inform the Persians of the laws and regulations which already governed the Egyptian society (Bedford 2001).

Ska, focusing more on the biblical texts, likewise claims that the textual support for Frei's 'Persian authorization theory', cited above, does not stand up to further scrutiny (Ska 2001: 164–7). Turning to the Pentateuch itself, Ska highlights that it contains much material that any Persian interested in local law would frown upon. Why, for example, are there so many narrative texts (e.g. all of Genesis) if the Pentateuch aimed to be a Persian legal document? Moreover, the inner contradictions render the Pentateuch less than useful for legislative purposes (Ska 2001: 168–9). Finally, the fact that the Pentateuch is written in Hebrew rather than in Aramaic does not suggest any external body of control; rather the community in Yehud was eager to establish solid links with its own past (Ska 2001: 170). Instead of any imperial authorization model, Ska suggests that the Pentateuch is better seen as containing the 'official and national archives/library' of the Second Temple community, which contains documents about Israel's origins and juridical organization (Ska 2001: 170–9).

Blenkinsopp likewise is more sceptical as to the Persian role in the compilation of the Pentateuch than Frei. The Persian authorities may have served as the impetus for the codification of the Pentateuchal law yet, as Blenkinsopp highlights, there is no real evidence to suggest that they oversaw it. In fact, it is actually extremely unlikely that the Persian authorities monitored the compilation of the religious literature of the numerous people under their control (Blenkinsopp 2001: 60–2).

Grabbe concurs. After his detailed discussion of the extra-biblical texts germane to the issue (the Passover Decree from Elephantine, the correspondence about the Elephantine YHW temple, the Udjahorresne Inscription, the Susa Statue of Darius, the Xanthus Trilingual Inscription, the Gadatas Inscription, and the Persepolis Inscription), he argues that there is little foundation behind the idea that it was Persian policy to fund and support religious cults and temples. In fact, apart from sanctuaries devoted to central deities, temples normally had to pay an imperial tax. There is no reason to assume that the Jerusalem temple would have been exempt from this duty. He further shows that while some evidence appears to suggest that the Persian bureaucracy would have responded favourably to a request from its subjects, it would normally have been dealt with by a satrap/governor rather than by the king himself. Furthermore, having a request granted did not automatically mean that funding was provided. Grabbe thus casts doubt upon the historicity of the Ezra account, insofar as it is highly unlikely that the Persian monarch would have given Ezra a substantial amount of money to spend on matters associated with Jewish law in Yehud (Grabbe 2001: 110–13).

We may then conclude that the available textual evidence does not fully confirm that the Persians were directly involved in the creation of the Pentateuch. At the same time, it is clear that they were involved in local affairs.

Ezra's Torah and the Pentateuch

An additional question pertains to the actual *content* of Ezra's Torah (Ezra 7.12, 14, 21, 26, plural also v. 25; Neh. 8). In particular, to what extent can it be equated with the Pentateuch that we have today? In Jewish tradition, Ezra is understood to be the one who restored the Law of Moses, as the earlier written copy had either been destroyed in the Babylonian sack of Jerusalem or fallen into oblivion (see ch. 5). A more critical approach needs to explore the allusions to and citations of Pentateuchal laws in Ezra-Nehemiah in order to reach an informed conclusion:

- Setting up an altar and offering sacrifices upon it (Ezra 3.2/Deut. 27.6-7)
- Establishment of daily offerings (Ezra 3.3, 5/Exod. 29.38-42; Num. 28.3-8)
- Duties of the priests and Levites (Ezra 6.18/Exod. 29; Lev. 8)
- Celebration of Passover (Ezra 6.19-22/Exod. 12.1-6, 19, 45; Lev. 23.5-6; Num. 9.3, 5)
- Prohibition of marriage with native women (Ezra 9.11-12; Neh. 10.31; 13.25/Deut. 7.3)

- Celebration of the Feast of Tabernacles (Neh. 8/Lev. 23, cf. Deut. 16.13-18)
- The tithe of tithes (Neh. 10.38-40/Num. 9.6-14)
- Exclusion from the community of certain ethnic categories (Neh. 13.1-2/Deut. 23.3-4)

As we can see, the regulations in Ezra-Nehemiah do not depend on a single source but appear to be informed by both P (the Priestly Source) and D (Deuteronomy), that is, two of the sources traditionally thought to underlie the Pentateuch. This opens the question as to whether we can determine if a specific textual strand in Ezra-Nehemiah might be closely aligned with a particular Pentateuchal source. For example, the particular author of Nehemiah 8 may have been more familiar with P than with D: Neh. 8.18 and Lev. 23.39-43 agree that Israel shall build booths and live in them for *eight* days; Deut. 16.13-16 mentions only *seven* days. In other cases, no clear pattern emerges. It may therefore be fair to conclude with Blenkinsopp that 'it is tolerably clear that the author of Ezra 7 was familiar with what is now known as Deuteronomistic and Priestly legislation', and that Ezra's Torah corresponds to the legal content of the Pentateuch at 'a mature but not yet final stage of evolution' (Blenkinsopp 2001: 56–7, 59–60; Grabbe 2001: 94–5, 99).

Grabbe further discusses the attested occurrences of the phrase 'the Law of Moses'. He highlights that the concept of a 'Law of Moses' is not found throughout the entire Pentateuch, but is confined to the book of Deuteronomy. Outside the Pentateuch, it appears in the DtrH and in the Chronicler's account. The book of Joshua contains the phrase several times (Josh. 1.8; 8.31-32, 34; 23.6), as well as the phrase 'the book of the Torah of God' (Josh. 24.26). The term is also used in 1 Kings 2.3 in the context of David's instruction to Solomon. In other cases, it appears to refer to the specific book of Deuteronomy (2 Kings 14.6 quoting Deut. 24.16). Lastly, the phrase is used in the context of Josiah's reform, commonly understood to be associated with the book of Deuteronomy (2 Kings 22.8, 11, 16; 23.2, 21, 24-25) (Grabbe 2001: 97). The evidence from the book of Chronicles is more diverse. In many cases, the phrase appears in the context of the cult, the priests and the temple, where matters should be carried out in accordance with 'the (book of the) Torah of YHWH/Moses' (1 Chron. 16.40; 2 Chron. 17.9; 23.18; 30.16; 31.3-4). Other cases are more general (1 Chron. 22.12; 2 Chron. 25.4; 33.8). Finally, the phrase 'Torah of Moses' is attested in Mal. 4.4 [Heb. 3.22] and Dan. 9.11 and 13 (Grabbe 2001: 97). According to Grabbe, while the Pentateuch in all likelihood reached its present shape in the Persian period, we do not need to give historical credence to the account in Ezra 7, nor must we think that Ezra was responsible for the compilation of the Torah (Grabbe 2001: 111–13).

Who ruled Yehud: The governor or the priest?

Given the importance of the temple and the Torah in post-monarchic Yehud, combined with the lack of political independence, the question has risen to what extent fifth-century Yehud might be called a 'temple-state'. Weinberg in particular, speaks of Yehud as a 'citizen-temple community' (*Bürger-Tempel-Gemeinde*), that is, a socioeconomic unit which is defined by its religious affiliation to a temple. According to Weinberg, the temple, ruled by its clergy, controlled the economy of Yehud. Weinberg maintains that the post-monarchic society changed its structure. In the new situation without a nation, the unit called 'the fathers' house' became the new basic social unit in the society. The leaders of the individual 'houses' played a central role in the society, and the High Priest stood at the top of the local hierarchy. The imperial Persian administration had granted local power to the temple and its leader, deeming the clergy to be the most loyal to the imperial interests (Weinberg 1992: e.g. 49–61, 122, 126).

Weinberg's proposal has not gone unchallenged. Williamson, for example, has pointed out that Weinberg takes the existence of a citizen-temple community for granted rather than actually arguing for it on the basis of firm textual evidence (Williamson 1995). More recently, Cataldo has challenged Weinberg's claim that Yehud constituted a theocracy, claiming that it is based on an uncritical reading of the biblical material and does not rest on any extra-biblical evidence (Cataldo 2009: 19–22). Looking at four case studies of alleged theocracies (Maya, Yathrib/Medina, Geneva at the time of Calvin, and post-revolution Iran) in order to establish what characterizes a theocracy, Cataldo defines a theocracy as a 'social-political context governed by a dominant religious institution or authority that holds authority over and administers the social, economic, and political spheres or realms of a society' (Cataldo 2009: 166). Based on this definition, Cataldo concludes that post-monarchic Yehud cannot rightly be called a theocracy. Instead, it resembles more the situation in sixteenth-century Geneva where religious texts and ceremonies were used as propaganda or as vehicles for social protest, but where the Church rulers did not govern over the social, economic spheres of the society and political realms. There is furthermore, contrary to Weinberg's claim, little evidence that the High Priest had any authority over the social or political spheres of the society (Cataldo 2009: 170–92). Bedford agrees with Cataldo as he stresses the relative political weakness of the priesthood. On the basis of the material in Nehemiah and corroborated by that in the Haggai-Malachi corpus, the political power of the priesthood in post-monarchic Yehud was limited to affairs which directly referred to the temple and its cult. The governor had markedly more power and the priests deferred to him (Bedford 2015: 342–6).

Bibliography of key studies

Bedford, Peter R. 'Temple Funding and Priestly Authority in Achaemenid Judah', in Jonathan Stökl and Caroline Waerzeggers (eds), *Exile and Return: The Babylonian Context* (BZAW, 478; Berlin: de Gruyter, 2015), pp. 336–51.

Briant, Pierre. *From Cyrus to Alexander: A History of the Persian Empire*, trans. Peter T. Daniels (Winona Lake, IN: Eisenbraun, 2002).

Cataldo, Jeremiah. W. *A Theocratic Yehud? Issues of Government in a Persian Province* (LHBOTS, 498; T&T Clark: New York, 2009).

Dandamayev, Muhammad. 'Achaemenid Imperial Policies and Provincial Governments', *Iranica Antiqua* 34 (1999), pp. 269–82.

Faust, Avraham. *Judah in the Neo-Babylonian Period: The Archaeology of Desolation* (Archaeology and Biblical Studies, 18; Atlanta, GA: SBL, 2012).

Fried, Lisbeth S. *The Priest and the Great King: Temple-Palace Relations in the Persian Empire* (Biblical and Judaic Studies from the University of California, San Diego, 10; Winona Lake, IN: Eisenbrauns, 2004).

Hoglund, Kenneth G. *Achaemenid Imperial Administration in Syria-Palestine and the Missions of Ezra and Nehemiah* (SBLDS, 125; Atlanta, GA: Scholars Press, 1992).

Knoppers, Gary N. and Lester L. Grabbe with Deirdre Fulton (eds). *Exile and Restoration Revisited: Essays on the Babylonian and Persian Periods in Memory of Peter R. Ackroyd* (LSTS, 73; London: T&T Clark, 2009).

Lipschits, Oded and Manfred Oeming (eds), *Judah and the Judeans in the Persian Period* (Winona Lake, IN: Eisenbrauns, 2006).

Watts, James W. (ed.). *Persia and Torah: The Theory of Imperial Authorization of the Pentateuch* (SBL Symposium Series, 17: Atlanta, GA: SBL, 2001).

Weinberg, Joel. *The Citizen-Temple Community*, trans. Daniel L. Smith-Christopher (JSOTS, 151; Sheffield: Sheffield Academic Press, 1992).

4

The Marriage Crisis

The final two chapters in Ezra (Ezra 9–10) and the final section in Nehemiah (Neh. 13.23-32) speak of what is often called 'the marriage crisis', that is, a situation where Jewish men had married foreign women and where Ezra and Nehemiah plead with/force these men to divorce these women, thus leaving their former wives and their shared children homeless. This behaviour must have caused severe hardship to the people involved and has thus often been criticized by exegetes. To quote Japhet: 'The radicalism and severity of this proposal is glaring: it would cause the breaking up of families, the tearing of children from their fathers, the breaching of marriage contracts, the maltreatment of the weaker components of the Judean society – that is, women and children – and would cause a general social unrest and emotional suffering' (Japhet 2007: 144).

Many issues arise from these actions of historical, theological and ethical significance. As elsewhere in this study, two interrelated issues exist, namely, one historical and one literary. Beginning with the former, why was it so important for the community of returned exiles in Yehud to keep themselves apart and not to mix with the people who had remained in the land during the Neo-Babylonian period? Turning to the literary question, why were the mixed marriages so important to the authors of Ezra-Nehemiah that they mentioned them twice in strategic key locations: first, at the end of Ezra, and then again at the very end of Nehemiah?

The danger of intermarriage in Yehud

Our present discussion focuses on the historical question. This question assumes that the pertinent material in Ezra 9–10 and Neh. 13.23-32 reflects the concerns of the community of returned exiles in Yehud in the fifth century BCE, an assumption that is entirely reasonable. As noted in ch. 2, much of the material in Ezra-Nehemiah is likely to stem from that time. Moreover, the texts shed light upon their authors' world views and, as such, have historical significance.

Scholars have so far understood the marriage crisis in Ezra 9–10 in five ways (Southwood 2012: 73–122). They are all to a certain extent interconnected; the question is more where the emphasis lies.

1 A matter of apostasy

A number of scholars argue that Ezra (and Nehemiah) wished to expel the foreign women because he feared that these women would lead the people of Yehud into idolatry. The danger is real, insofar as children often tend to adopt their mother's religious customs and beliefs (Fensham 1982: 124). This interpretation is supported by the inter-textual link to Deut. 7.1-4/Exod. 34.11-16 in Ezra 9.1-2. According to this line of interpretation, the main issue at stake is the *religious* identity of the community. Ezra 9–10 would thus reflect a conflict in Yehud between Ezra, the spokesman for a (small) group within Yehud with a narrowly defined understanding of their religious identity, up against the surrounding inhabitants who defined their religious identity in a different way (Blenkinsopp 1988: 175–7). At the same time, other factors speak against it. In particular, if the issue was only their religious affiliation, why were the women not offered the option of conversion, that is, to adopt their husbands' religious identity (Southwood 2012: 78)? That this could be done is exemplified most clearly in the book of Ruth (cf. Isa. 56.1-8) (Japhet 2007: 154).

2 A matter of inheritance and land tenure

Ezra 9–10 speaks of Jewish *men* who have married foreign *women*. Is this gender division a salient point? Notably, Ezra does not speak of Jewish women who have married foreign men (note, however, that Neh. 10.30 conveys a more balanced notion). This imbalance is characteristic of the entire Hebrew Bible, the aforementioned book of Ruth being a case in point. Does this gender imbalance reflect a real social situation or male-centred concerns or both?

This question leads us to the second common explanation of the forced divorces in Ezra 9–10, namely, that they reflect the fear of loss of inheritance: the forced divorces sought to make sure that the land of Yehud would not leave Jewish ownership. If women could inherit property, then foreign wives turned widows who, in turn, remarried men from their community of birth would endanger the rights of the Jewish community to their ancestral land (Eskenazi 1992: 35; Washington 1994: 232–8). This view is, however, problematic for several reasons, not the least because it is counter-intuitive. If the issue really was inheritance, and if women really could inherit land, we would expect the reverse gender imbalance. The fear would instead be that foreign men would marry Jewish women without living brothers (Southwood 2012: 79).

The issue of property can nevertheless be understood to have caused the forced divorces when seen from the assumed conflict between the returnees and those who had remained in the land. The returning exiles may have considered their ancestral land to be their property, as would the people who in the meantime had acquired and worked the land. This interpretation assumes that the foreign women were not really foreign; rather they were simply Judahite women who had never been to Babylon. Douglas, for example, envisions a sharp division in the Judahite society between, on the one hand, the 'separatists', that is, the returnees led by Ezra and Nehemiah, and the 'unifiers', led by the priests who wished to create a more open society which included those who had remained in the land (Douglas 2002).

Along slightly different lines, some scholars have suggested that Ezra and Nehemiah had certain obligations towards the Persian monarch who had commissioned them. According to Kessler, Ezra and Nehemiah were to re-establish a community and a central shrine in Yehud, all subject to a shared version of the worship of YHWH and in subjection to and with the support of the Persian Crown. This group consisted of a single, ethnically well-defined group, that is, the returning exiles. The intermarriages violated their task to keep the land in the hands of this well-defined group which, in turn, caused them to enforce the divorces (Kessler 2006: 106, 110–12; cf. Hoglund 1992: 223, 231–40).

This view is problematic insofar as it places (too) much emphasis on the historical imperial appointment of Ezra which may or may not be justified. It further rests on very little textual support as nothing in Ezra 9–10 (or Neh. 13.23-32) mentions a connection between the imperial appointment and the forced divorces.

Finally, the notion of property may have provided a legal loophole which enabled the expulsion of the foreign women. According to Japhet, the language in Ezra 9–10 suggests that the 'private, whimsical idea', made by Shechaniah during his conversation with Ezra, created the possibility of reducing the women's status from being wives to being concubines. As the latter, they would not really have been married to their Jewish husbands; instead the women were their men's property. There would thus be no need for a divorce. Moreover, the children of the union would not be classified as the men's sons and daughters, but instead take their mother's status of slave/property (Japhet 2007).

3   A matter of status, class and money

Who were the elite in Yehud in the fifth century BCE: the people who had remained in the land or the returning exiles? This question hinges on two interconnected issues, namely, wealth and status. Did the *Golah* group (i.e. the people who returned to Yehud from Babylon) who traced their lineage back to pre-exilic men of power also hold key leadership positions in post-exilic Yehud (Tiemeyer 2015: 68–72), or did they rather have less status and wealth than their indigenous counterparts (Smith-Christopher 1994: 256, 260–1)?

Smith-Christopher in particular has argued that the marriage crisis as portrayed in Ezra-Nehemiah does not fit with the notion that the returning exiles constituted a privileged elite. In view of this, he advances what we might call the 'hypergamy' theory. The phenomenon that we observe in Ezra-Nehemiah is thus that of success- or status-minded exilic men whose marriages to women from Yehud should be understood as an attempt to 'marry up' and thus to climb the social ladder. This would explain why the priests – who should have been the very people most passionate to uphold the boundaries of separation – were the ones who had married the 'foreign women' (Smith-Christopher 1994: 257). This theory gains additional support from the material in Nehemiah which testifies to a 'network of relationships cemented by *marriages de convenance*' between Sanballat and Tobiah on the one hand, and important elements of the aristocracy in Jerusalem on the other (Smith-Christopher 1994: 259). This theory shares certain key aspects with the aforementioned theory by Douglas in the sense that the priestly leadership sided with the indigenous population rather than with the *Golah* group.

The economic situation in Yehud has already been discussed in ch. 3. It bears repeating, though, that the available archaeological data do not suggest a wealthy Yehud. On the contrary, in view of Faust's discussion of the economic and demographic situation in Yehud (Faust 2012: 119–47), it is doubtful that the *Golah* group would have married the indigenous inhabitants of Yehud for the sake of the latter group's wealth. As to the economic status of the *Golah* group, we are left to speculate. Did the people with money leave Babylon because they were in the economic position to do so, or was it rather the people without money who left, because they saw a new opportunity in their ancestral homeland? Furthermore, this theory runs the risk of reducing the expressed religious concerns expressed by the text to socioeconomic factors (Southwood 2012: 87–8).

4 A matter of purity

Another common interpretation connects the marriage crisis with issues of purity and holiness. Milgrom, for example, maintains that Israel at this point had come to be viewed as a *sanctum* which ran the constant risk of pollution. Any adulteration of the 'holy seed' would thus be understood as a 'desecration', a term used frequently in Ezra 9–10 (9.2, 4; 10.2, 6, 10), that is, a trespassing across the border between holy and profane matters. The only way to restore Israel's purity would be via a 'sacrifice of expiation' (cf. Lev. 5.15), a term employed in Ezra 10.19 (Milgrom 1976: 71–3). The idea is developed further by Boda who argues that this theology is revealed in the preserved post-monarchic penitential prayers. He detects the notion of pollution and expiation in the penitential prayer in Ezra 9 and in the community's prayer in Nehemiah 9 (Boda 2006). The rationale behind the expulsion of the foreign women would thus be to preserve the purity and holiness of the people of Israel.

Other scholars challenge the view that Ezra-Nehemiah is concerned primarily with *ritual* purity and argue instead that what is at stake here is *moral* purity. Notably, Klawans maintains that purity here serves as a metaphor for moral and religious behaviour. The foreign women constitute a danger inasmuch as they are 'inherently idolatrous' (Klawans 1998: 401) and thus would lead the Israelites into sin. In support of this interpretation, Klawans points out that the remedy is not ritual purification of the community but permanent expulsion of the women (Klawans 1998: 398–402). While this is a possible interpretation, it should be noted that the vocabulary used in Ezra 9–10 is ritual in character (Southwood 2012: 91).

Other scholars connect the concept of purity and ethnicity, arguing that holiness is biological in the sense that it is transmitted through Israelite descent. Hayes, for instance, demonstrates that the ban on intermarriage was not motivated by a fear of contracting any form of ritual impurity from a Gentile; rather it was motivated by the fear of profaning the community by giving birth to children with 'impure' blood. This new type of impurity is sinful, contagious and irreversible (Hayes 1999: 6–14; cf. Harrington 2008: 106–11, 116). Along similar lines yet expressed differently by Olyan, Ezra-Nehemiah employs the ideology of purity to delineate the border between the community and 'the Other' (Olyan 2004).

From a different perspective, Janzen maintains that Ezra 9–10, using the vocabulary of holy versus impure, is ultimately about separating Israel from the neighbouring people. Using the term 'witch-hunt', Janzen argues that the foreign women were selected to be the scapegoats and chased away in order to enforce the moral order and thus to strengthen the social order. The divorces were thus a 'ritualized act of purification'. These types of witch hunt are often triggered by a crisis, whereby the society responds by seeking to delineate who is really a member and who is an outsider (Janzen 2002; 2008).

5 A matter of identity

A growing number of scholars, among them Zlotan-Sivan, connect Ezra's actions in Ezra 9–10 with issues of Jewish identity. In her comparative study of Ezra's approach to intermarriage and that found in the Roman Empire, Zlotan-Sivan highlights the links between citizenship and marriage. Through marriage, a woman would be able to claim her husband's ethnic identity. While the Roman legislation encouraged integration through marriage, Ezra and Nehemiah went the opposite way. Ezra sought to expel the foreign women in order to reinforce his own definition of what it means to be 'Jewish' and to curtail other interpretations. Ezra's arguments appear to be based on earlier traditions while they in reality are new and revolutionary. Zlotan-Sivan concludes that 'Romans are made, Jews are born' (Slotan-Sivan 2000). This interpretation focuses less on the women themselves and more on the children of the intermarriages who were, along with their mothers, expelled. If the marriages had been accepted, then these children would have had Jewish 'citizenship' in the sense of Jewish status/identity.

Along similar lines, Johnson argues that identity issues, rather than racial issues, lie behind the ban on intermarriages in Ezra-Nehemiah. In her view, the ban on intermarriage was brought about by the trauma, triggered by the exilic experiences of the small and struggling community, and aimed at securing its identity. The marriages themselves, understood by Johnson to have been between Jewish men of power and high-ranking Persian women, had been forged for reasons of economy and status (Johnson 2011: 15).

Moffat's monograph follows suit insofar as Moffat maintains that the ban on intermarriage is rooted in a crisis of identity. This crisis stemmed in part from the meeting of the returning exiles with the people of the land, both of which called themselves 'Israel', and it was augmented by the fact that both 'Israels' formed a minority group under foreign, Persian rule (Moffat 2013). To safeguard their identity, the *Golah* community established identity markers. It is, however, incorrect to make any sharp distinction between religious and racial markers. Rather, genealogical descent, shared exilic experience, and common religious practices together served to shape the *Golah* identity (Moffat 2013: 79–82).

Heger agrees with this view as well. He offers a substantial counter-argument to the above-mentioned 'moral' interpretations of Hayes and others, stating that Ezra's ban on intermarriage did not primarily seek to preserve the holy seed from intermixing with the profane seed (of Gentiles). Rather, in his view, the prime concern of Ezra's community was to ensure the survival of the Israelite people among the idolatrous surrounding nations which threatened to overwhelm them. In other words, the ban on marriage was motivated by cultural and religious concerns rather than by any genealogical purity. In the new post-monarchic era where the identity of Israel could no longer be ensured through political means, Israel's survival as a distinct people came to depend on a sharp separation between Israel and the rest of the world (Heger 2014: 312–16).

5.1 A matter of ethnicity

The previous section explored the wider concept of identity. The studies that fall into this section look at a related issue, namely, that of ethnicity. Identity and ethnicity are two distinct concepts, yet when speaking about the identity of the returnees, ethnicity can be understood as a subcategory of identity. The returnees understood their identity to be informed by and in line with their ethnicity. In many cases, ethnic groups understand their own identity by the help of boundaries that distinguishes them from other people. Ethnicity is in this sense about setting boundaries and determining who is 'in' and who is 'the Other'. Some kinds of interaction between the in-group and the out-groups are allowed while others are forbidden. Very often, intermarriage with the out-group counts among the latter, forbidden actions. It is understood to be important to uphold the group's distinctiveness. This distinctiveness can be several things: a common proper name to identify the group, a myth of common ancestry, shared historical memories, a common culture, a link to a homeland and a general sense of solidarity (Hutchinson and Smith 1996: 7).

Southwood's study focuses on the specific issue of ethnicity. Looking at the issue through the lens of ethnicity and return migration, she argues that the marriage crisis in Ezra-Nehemiah serves to preserve Israel's identity/ethnicity which had become endangered by return migration. The biblical text reflects the culture shock felt by a group of Jewish exiles upon their re-migration to Yehud, and the proscribed divorces are the symptoms of their deeper feelings of alienation upon realizing that their ancestral homeland is different from what they had imagined and that the people living in it resemble the strangers in whose midst they had lived when in exile (Southwood 2012).

5.2 A matter of exile

Continuing with the matter of identity, a few scholars have argued that the determining factor to Jewish identity which, according to Ezra and Nehemiah, gave a person a passport to the community was the shared *exilic experience*. Only those people who had been to Babylon would be eligible for citizenship in the new Yehud. Spark, for example, explicitly states that for many, the exilic community and their supporters in Yehud maintained that *only* the exilic community formed the real Israel. In response to the threat of losing their homeland to the Judahite community, the exiles came up with the notion that group membership required participation in the exilic experience itself (cf. Ezek. 11.14-21) (Spark 1998: 288, 314–15).

5.3 A matter of narrative

Texts are central to identity formation. A community may choose older texts and reinterpret them to fit the needs of the community, or it may create new texts which serve the same purpose. Texts which create a shared past can influence the present. A shared past can shape a national identity, even if what is shared is a textual tradition rather than an actual historical event. This endeavour can be called 'narrativization' and consists of three main components. The group *selects* specific individual events out of the entirety of history and attributes special importance to them. They then *plot* a coherent narrative by arranging these events in a particular order and assign to them a narrative role. Finally, they *interpret* this sequence of events in a particular way and determine how it has shaped the identity of the group (Cornell 2000: 43).

Esler tackles the issue of identity by focusing on the role of narrative in identity formation. It is less about the actual historical experience and more about the narrative about that experience. The exiles in Babylon had needed to establish boundaries between themselves and the surrounding people in order to survive as a group. Upon their migration to Yehud, they needed to reconstruct anew or reinvent their ethnic identity. They created a story which emphasized the shared identity of all those who had experienced the exile. This narrative, in turn, served to uphold the border between the 'insiders' and the 'outsiders' and thus to delimit the identity of the 'insiders' (Esler 2003: 417–18).

A narrative about the past does not necessarily need to be true. A notable example is the idea of the Scottish clan tartans with distinct patterns. Although it can be shown that tartan cloths reached Scotland only in the sixteenth century from Flanders, the idea of clan colours nevertheless featured prominently in the establishment of a distinct, modern Scottish identity (Trevor-Roper 1983). What is important is the *ideas* about the past and the power of books to shape, legitimize and spread these ideas. In the specific case of ancient Israel, Weeks notes that the survival of individuals after the destruction of Judah and Jerusalem in 586 BCE does not in itself explain their survival as a distinct group and their hope for political restoration. What was needed was some means of telling these individuals that they belonged together. Weeks further highlights the importance of

Israel's textual heritage, as he shows that the returning exiles founded their claim of a separate identity on authoritative texts and that this textual focus, in turn, gave rise to the creation of new texts (Weeks 2002).

Bibliography of key studies

Douglas, Mary. 'Responding to Ezra: The Priests and the Foreign Wives', *Biblical Interpretation* 10 (2002), pp. 1–23.

Eskenazi, Tamara C. 'Out of the Shadows: Biblical Women in the Postexilic Era', *JSOT* 54 (1992), pp. 25–43.

Esler, Philip F. 'Ezra-Nehemiah as a Narrative of (Re-Invented) Israelite Identity', *Biblical Interpretation* 11, no. 3 (2003), pp. 413–26.

Heger, Paul. *Women in the Bible, Qumran, and Early Rabbinic Literature: Their Status and Roles* (STDJ, 110; Leiden: Brill, 2014).

Janzen, David. *Witch-hunts, Purity and Social Boundaries: The Expulsion of the Foreign Women in Ezra 9–10* (JSOTS, 350; Sheffield: Sheffield Academic Press, 2002).

Japhet, Sara. 'The Expulsion of the Foreign Women (Ezra 9–10): The Legal Basis, Precedents, and Consequences for the Definition of Jewish Identity', in Friedhelm Hartenstein and Michael Pietsch (eds), '*Sieben Augen auf einem Stein*' *(Sach 3,9): Studien zur Literatur des Zweiten Temples. Festschrift für Ina Willi-Plein zum 65. Geburtstag* (Neukirchen-Vluyn: Neukirchener Verlag, 2007), pp. 141–61.

Johnson, Willa M. *The Holy Seed Has Been Defiled: The Interethnic Marriage Dilemma in Ezra 9–10* (HBM, 33; Sheffield: Sheffield Phoenix Press, 2011).

Kessler, John. 'Persia's Loyal Yahwists: Power Identity and Ethnicity in Achaemenid Yehud', in Oded. Lipschits and Manfred Oeming (eds), *Judah and the Judeans in the Persian Period* (Winona Lake, IN: Eisenbrauns, 2006), pp. 91–121.

Klawans, Jonathan. 'Idolatry, Incest, and Impurity: Moral Defilement in Ancient Judaism', *JSJ* 29, no. 4 (1998), pp. 391–415.

Milgrom, Jacob. *Cult and Conscience: The Asham and the Priestly Doctrine of Repentance* (SJLA, 18; Leiden: Brill, 1976).

Moffat, Donald P. *Ezra's Social Drama: Identity Formation, Marriage and Social Conflict in Ezra 9 and 10* (LHBOTS, 579; London: T&T Clark, 2013).

Olyan, Saul M. 'Purity Ideology in Ezra-Nehemiah as a Tool to Reconstitute the Community', *JSJ* 35, no. 1 (2004), pp. 1–16.

Slotan-Sivan, H. 'The Silent Woman of Yehud: Notes on Ezra 9–10', *JJS* 51 (2000), pp. 3–18.

Smith-Christopher, David L. 'The Mixed Marriage Crisis in Ezra 9–10 and Nehemiah 13: A Study of the Sociology of the Post-exilic Judean Community', in Tamara C. Eskenazi and Kent H. Richards (eds), *Second Temple Studies 2: Temple and Community in the Persian Period* (JSOTS, 175; Sheffield, England: JSOT Press, 1994), pp. 243–65.

Southwood, Katherine E. *Ethnicity and the Mixed Marriage Crisis in Ezra 9–10: An Anthropological Approach* (OTM; Oxford: Oxford University Press, 2012).

Spark, Kenton L. *Ethnicity and Identity in Ancient Israel: Prolegomena to the Study of Ethnic Sentiments and their Expression in the Hebrew Bible* (Winona Lake, IN: Eisenbrauns, 1998).

Washington, H. C. 'The Strange Women of Proverbs 1–9 and Post-Exilic Society', in Tamara C. Eskenazi and Kent H. Richards (eds), *Second Temple Studies 2: Temple and Community in the Persian Period* (JSOTS, 175; Sheffield, England: JSOT Press, 1994), pp. 217–42.

Weeks, Stuart D. E. 'Biblical Literature and the Emergence of Ancient Jewish Nationalism', *Biblical Interpretation* 10 (2002), pp. 144–57.

5

Ezra-Nehemiah in its Later Reception

The reception of Ezra-Nehemiah in Judaism and Christianity is a fascinating tale. The matter begins already in the two canons. In the Masoretic Text (MT), Ezra-Nehemiah appears in the *Ketuvim* (the writings). In contrast, Ezra-Nehemiah is situated in the Septuagint (LXX) among the 'Historical Books' after Chronicles and before Esther. This positioning of the text has repercussions for how readers have understood and appreciated the material.

Ezra-Nehemiah features a number of characters. Some of them, such as the Persian monarchs, are clearly historical men. Other figures, such as Zerubbabel and Joshua, appear not only in Ezra-Nehemiah but also elsewhere in the Hebrew Bible. These two men, alongside Sheshbazzar, are important characters in the drama of Ezra 1–6 as leaders of the group of returning exiles. Who were these men, what role did they play in history, and what function do they have in Ezra-Nehemiah? The following journey through the reception history of Ezra-Nehemiah will focus on the characterization of three of the main characters – Zerubabbel, Ezra and Nehemiah – but also explore other characters, among them Sheshbazzar, Joshua and Sanballat.

Haggai, Zechariah 1–6 and Ezra 1–6

Zerubbabel and Joshua are known from Haggai and Zechariah 1–6. Zerubbabel is titled 'governor of Yehud' and his Davidic lineage is emphasized in these texts. He is envisioned as playing an important role in the rebuilding of the temple (Hag. 1.1, 12, 14; 2.2, 4, 21-23; Zech. 4.6aβ-10a). Joshua is likewise considered to be a significant character in Yehud, titled 'High Priest' and put in charge of the temple (Hag. 1.1, 12, 14; 2.2, 4; Zech. 3; 6.9-15). In my view, it is reasonably clear that we are dealing with two historical persons who were involved in the affairs of Yehud during the reign of Darius I. Moreover, I see no reason to doubt that Zerubbabel served as the local governor at this time.

Zerubbabel's political role is downplayed in Ezra 1–6. He is mentioned without his official title and Davidic pedigree, presumably as part of an attempt to stress the political status quo in Yehud under Persian rule: nobody had any aspirations towards independence. At the same time, Ezra 1–6 depicts Zerubbabel as having been involved in the affairs of Yehud for a considerable period of time, standing at the head of the community throughout the long process of rebuilding the temple (Japhet 1982: 68–89).

Turning to the more enigmatic character, Sheshbazzar, he appears only in Ezra 1.8, 11 and Ezra 5.16. He is called 'prince' and the laying of the foundation of the temple is attributed to him. This raises the pertinent issue: did Sheshbazzar or Zerubbabel build the temple? One way out of the conundrum is to assume that these two names really denote *one* man, but this assumption lacks textual support. The alternative is to argue that the foundation of the temple was actually laid twice, first by Sheshbazzar during the reign of Cyrus, and then again by Zerubbabel during the reign of Darius I.

1 Esdras

1 Esdras (see ch. 2) assigns more power and influence to Zerubbabel than what its canonical counterpart does. In addition to the biblical material of 2 Chron. 35.1–36.23; Ezra 1–10; and Neh. 7.72–8.23, this book contains a story about King Darius's three body guards, one of whom is Zerubbabel. While Haggai and Zechariah together portray Zerubbabel as a Davidic figure of royal dimension (esp. Hag. 2.20-23; Zech. 4.6aβ-10a), Ezra 1–6 downplays his role (Japhet 1982: 68–94). 1 Esdras seeks to rectify this situation by giving Zerubbabel a backstory, as well as an alibi and a reason for not being in Jerusalem when the temple building came to a halt.

In contrast, the description of the character of Ezra in 1 Esdras corresponds to a large degree with that which is found in the canonical book of Ezra, with the important exception that the narrative moves immediately from the people's mass divorce (Ezra 10) to Ezra's public reading of the law (Nehemiah 8). It should also be noted that 1 Esdras omits the whole Nehemiah story. The character of Nehemiah does not appear and none of his actions (rebuilding of the walls, his reforms) are mentioned. It also omits the covenant renewal ceremony.

On the whole, 1 Esdras has a different and more optimistic theology than the canonical Ezra-Nehemiah. The already purified people hear the law and there is no opportunity of backsliding (Fried 2014: 58–61).

The Dead Sea Scrolls

The textual evidence from Qumran of Ezra-Nehemiah consists of two small fragments found in Cave 4. These fragments contain parts of the texts of Ezra 4.2-6, 9-11, and 5.17–6.5. They follow the MT with a few very minor differences in terms of spelling and in terms of verbal form (Ezra 6.1 reads 'they searched' [3m.pl.] while 4QEzra reads 'he searched' [3m.sg.]). Very recently, another fragment from Neh. 3.14-15 was discovered (Harrington 2011: 251, fn. 1). This relative lack of manuscripts does not, however, necessarily imply that Ezra-Nehemiah was unimportant in the Qumran community. On the contrary, as Harrington has discussed, there is a high degree of conceptual influence from Ezra-Nehemiah upon the scrolls found at the site (e.g. 4QMMT [the 'Halakhic Letter' or the 'Sectarian Manifesto'], the Temple Scroll, the Damascus Document) on the particular topic of intermarriage, as can be seen in the ban on marriage to outsiders advocated by many of the sectarian texts (Harrington 2011).

Josephus

The Jewish historian Josephus, living in the first century CE, recounts the time of the Restoration (from Cyrus to the death of Alexander the Great) in his book *Antiquities of the Jews* (*Ant.* 11). He based much of his historical writings on 1 Esdras (Fried 2014: 4, 61–4), but it is also possible that he had other material at his disposal which provided him with (not necessarily reliable) information about the Persian period (Grabbe 1987). Here, we shall explore how Josephus portrayed the three characters of Ezra, Nehemiah, and Zerubbabel

Beginning with Ezra, Josephus does not devote as much time to Ezra as he does to most of the other key biblical characters (Abraham, Isaac, Jacob, Joseph, etc.). Nothing is made of his high priestly genealogy and little is made of his learning. It is possible that Josephus wished to emphasize Ezra's subordination to Moses: he was a teacher of obedience to the Law but not on a par with Moses. Josephus further stresses Ezra's loyalty to his ruler and his endeavour to uphold law and order (by implication, the Jews' loyalty to the Empire). According to Feldman, this portrayal would have appealed to the Romans who emphasized obedience to the law. In fact, Ezra in Josephus' hands becomes more of a competent and effective (political) leader than a religious teacher (Feldman 1993; 2001: 231–42).

Turning to Nehemiah, Josephus is even less interested in him. This may in part be due to the fact that Josephus's account depends to a large extent on 1 Esdras, where Nehemiah does not appear (see above). Josephus portrays him as a dynamic, well-organized and persuasive secular leader and as a man respectful of the law, and he emphasizes Nehemiah's loyalty to the Persian monarch as well as the latter's confidence in Nehemiah's ability. To bolster this picture, Josephus elaborates on the opposition that Nehemiah faces in Yehud and his fearless endurance of hardship (Feldman 2001: 241–7).

Finally, Josephus increases the significance of Zerubbabel. He writes that he was a friend of Darius I, and that he was appointed governor of the Jewish returnees (in line with Haggai and Zech. 1–6). He further incorporates and enhances the material from 1 Esdras about the competition during Darius I's reign, having the Persian king complimenting Zerubbabel on his wisdom and granting him safe conduct to Jerusalem to build the temple (*Ant.* 11.59, a change from 1 Esdras which speak of the rebuilding of the city [1 Esdr. 4.47]) (Feldman 2001: 249–50).

Ben Sira 49.11-13

Jesus Ben Sira, or Ecclesiasticus as he is also called, wrote his book around 200 BCE. He does not mention Ezra in his list of Israel's (male) heroes in 49.11-13; instead he writes about Zerubbabel, Joshua and Nehemiah. Ben Sira commemorates Zerubbabel as a signet ring (inspired by Hag. 2.23) who together with Joshua rebuilt the temple, and he remembers Nehemiah as the man who built the fallen walls (of Jerusalem) and erected gates and buildings. As Grabbe notes, this reference in Ben Sira does not need to be based on the present form of Ezra-Nehemiah. On the contrary, its portrayal of Zerubbabel does not draw from Ezra 1–6 but from the earlier book of Haggai.

It is an open question as to why Ben Sira does not mention Ezra (the only other major omission from his list is that of Daniel, even though the narratives about him in Dan. 1–6 were likely to have been in circulation at his time [cf. Grabbe 1998: 85–6]). Did he not know of Ezra, or did he not think that he was significant? Marttila offers a detailed survey of a wide array of scholarly suggestions: did Ben Sira have an anti-Levite bias, was he only interested in men who built things, did he not know about the Ezra traditions, did he dislike Ezra's particularism, had Ben Sira an aversion to reforms, did Ezra not fit Ben Sira's ideas of how the Aaronite priests should behave, was Ezra's role as a 'scribe' not what Ben Sira understood the term to be, or was it simply imprudent to speak of Ezra in Ben Sira's contemporary political climate of conflict within the clergy (Marttila 2012: 192–206)? The theories are many, and it is likely that Ben Sira's lack of reference to Ezra must remain a mystery.

2 Maccabees 1.18–2.15

Like Ben Sira, 2 Maccabees does not mention Ezra. It is also silent about Zerubbabel and Joshua, instead emphasizing the role of Nehemiah. Notably, 2 Macc. 1.18 states that Nehemiah built the temple and the altar.

The references to Nehemiah appear first in the form of a letter (2 Macc. 1. 10-36), written by Judas Maccabeus and some other men in Judah, calling for the celebration of the Feast of Tabernacles (1.18). Throughout this letter, Nehemiah is portrayed as a cultic leader who builds the temple, offers sacrifices (1.18) and supervises the clergy (1.19-23). He is further given the task, alongside that of the prophet Jeremiah, of bridging the gap between the first and the second temple and of ensuring continuity of worship. In addition, Nehemiah is associated with Jewish learning and of collecting sacred books about Israel's kings and prophet to the extent that he founded a library (2.13) (Fitzpatrick-McKinley 2008: 113–14).

It is fair to say that Nehemiah has replaced the other three protagonists in 2 Maccabees. He is the temple builder, the restorer of the city of Jerusalem and the preserver of Jewish tradition (Grabbe 1998: 88–9). It is possible that 2 Maccabees emphasized Nehemiah's role in order to liken its own hero Judas Maccabeus to this great hero of the past. As stated by Fitzpatrick-McKinley, Nehemiah 'bears all the traits of the kind of Jewish hero needed in Maccabean times', ready to be a role model for Judas Maccabeus (Fitzpatrick-McKinley 2008: 115).

The lack of references to Zerubbabel and Ezra suggests that the author(s) of 1 Maccabees drew only from the book of Nehemiah. This situation, in turn, may indicate that at one point Ezra and Nehemiah were separate books (cf. ch. 2), but the evidence is inconclusive.

Rabbinic Judaism

The figure of Ezra is greatly esteemed in rabbinical literature. In particular, his association with the Torah (Nehemiah 8) has given rise to a wealth of traditions. As the reader and expounder of the law, Ezra is often compared with Moses who is considered to be the law-giver par excellence (Porton 2001: 317–20; Fried 2014: 142–4). Rabbi Josi, for example, claims in the Babylonian Talmud that had Moses not preceded him, Ezra would have been worthy of receiving the written Torah (i.e. the Pentateuch) for Israel. Furthermore, Ezra is assigned the task of 'changing the letters' in the Torah, presumably from the proto-Hebrew script to the current Hebrew script (i.e. the Aramaic letters) (*b.san.* 21b–22a, cf. Porton 2001: 320–3). Also in the Babylonian Talmud, Rabbi Shimon ben Eleazar states that Ezra is held to be responsible for the Jewish tradition of dividing the Torah into portions, to be read annually each Sabbath in the synagogue (*b.meg.* 31b).

In parallel, Ezra is also associated with the oral law, that is, the legal material which according to Jewish tradition was given orally to Moses on Mt Sinai and then handed down and discussed through generations, finally to be committed to writing in the Mishnah and other rabbinical compilations. For example, a group of ten decrees is attributed to Ezra by the Jerusalem Talmud, most of them dealing with regulations regarding Jewish women (the so-called Ten Regulations of Ezra, see *y.meg.* 29a-b). Porten suggests that this connection may stem from the narrative in Ezra 9–10, where Ezra sends away the foreign wives (Porton 2001: 326–32; cf. Zeitlin 1917).

The Babylonian Talmud is interested in the authorship of Ezra-Nehemiah but there are conflicting statements. According to *b.baba batra* 15a, Ezra is the author of the book bearing his name (Ezra-Nehemiah), as well as of the genealogies in Chronicles (esp. 1 Chron. 1–9). The rest of Chronicles was compiled by Nehemiah. In contrast, *b.san.* 93b states that the entire book of Ezra was composed by Nehemiah. The book as a whole was not, however, called Nehemiah because, according to Rabbi Jeremiah ben Abba, Nehemiah claimed merit for himself (see Neh. 5.19, below).

Many texts extol Ezra's role as a priest, scholar, teacher, legislator, prophet and holy man and compare him with Moses. According to the Babylonian Talmud, Ezra reached such levels of holiness that he was able to pronounce the divine name YHWH (*b.yom.* 69b). The rabbis further enhance Ezra's priestly role, making it surpass that of both Aaron and Joshua. One *midrash* (a rabbinical story which seeks to resolve exegetical problems extant in a biblical passage) located in the collection of *midrashot* associated with the book of Ecclesiastes, claims that Ezra would have been High Priest even if he had been a contemporary of Aaron himself (*Koheleth Rabbah* 1.4).

Several *midrashot* explore why Ezra waited so long before he travelled to Yehud: Zerubbabel and Joshua had settled in Yehud already during the reign of Darius (see further Porton 2001: 314–17; Fried 2014: 140–1). Why did Ezra not participate in the rebuilding of the temple? Seeking to provide reasons/excuses for his lack of participation, one *midrash* explains that Ezra waited with his journey to Yehud until after Joshua's death lest the latter feel intimidated by Ezra's presence in the land (in view of Ezra's superior qualities) (*Song of Songs Rabba* 5.5; cf. Feldman 1993: 192, fn. 7). In parallel, another *midrash* maintains that Ezra tarried in Babylon because he did not wish to leave behind his teacher Baruch ben Neriah (Jeremiah's scribe) who by then was too old to travel (*b.meg.* 16b).

The Babylonian Talmud further identifies Ezra with the prophet Malachi. The necessity of putting away foreign wives (Mal. 2.10-11; Ezra 9–10) is the perceived link between the two characters (*b.meg.* 15a).

Finally, Ezra is considered to be the leader of the men who founded the so-called Great Assembly, a legendary institution of authority which is supposed to have existed in the post-monarchic period. The tradition tells how the Torah was handed down from Moses, via Joshua, the elders, and the prophets, to the 'men of the Great Assembly (*Abot* 1.1; see further Leuchter 2012: 341–4).

There is much less material about Nehemiah in rabbinical literature. The Babylonian Talmud claims that Zerubbabel (meaning 'seed of Babylon') was so called because he was 'sown' in Babylon; his real name was Nehemiah. This identification is based on the fact that the Bible labels both Zerubbabel and Nehemiah 'governor' of Yehud (*b.San.* 38a). It follows according to rabbinic interpretation that Nehemiah arrived in Yehud already in the sixth century BCE.

Nehemiah is significantly less popular, in part because of his habit of self-aggrandizement. In particular, what annoys many of the rabbis is Nehemiah's statement 'Remember me, o my God, with favour, because of all that I have done for this people' (Neh. 5.19). In particular, Nehemiah thought that his own good deeds would, in themselves, give him credits and make him deserving of God's compassion. As a result of Nehemiah's self-glorification, his book is not attributed to him but instead to Ezra (cf. above). Nehemiah's behaviour is further contrasted with that of David who made a similar request in Ps. 106.4. As David's request was a plea for God's mercy, however, the rabbis did not equate the two instances (*b.Sanh.* 93b; see also Rabinowitz 1990: 94–5).

The New Testament

In the New Testament (NT), there are extremely few references to the texts of Ezra-Nehemiah. The most important instance is 1 Cor. 5.1-2, where Paul suggests to the people of Corinth 'to mourn' over the incestuous man. This reference may allude to Ezra 10.6; Neh. 1.4; and 8.9. Notably, in Ezra 10.6, Ezra mourns over the faithlessness of the people (Ciampa and Rosner 2007: 706). The NT does not contain any explicit references to the characters of Ezra and Nehemiah. In contrast, Zerubbabel (mentioned in Ezra 3.2, 8; 5.2; Neh. 12:1, as well as in Haggai and Zechariah) appears in Jesus' genealogy in Lk. 3.27.

Ezra Apocalypse (4 Ezra)

In contrast, the so-called *Ezra Apocalypse/4 Ezra* (purportedly telling about the fall of Jerusalem in 586 BCE at the hands of the Neo-Babylonians) contains a significant amount of material about the character of Ezra. Ezra, an exile in Babylon, laments this disaster. He inquires of God how he could allow his precious city and his temple to be destroyed and his people to be handed over to the Babylonians, a people that are no better than the people of Israel. Ezra receives a number of (unsatisfactory) answers. He also sees a vision of the end-time when God will bring about the ultimate victory over evil.

4 Ezra 14 tells the story of how Ezra asks God for the spirit of holiness in order to write down the Law (which had been burnt at the time of the destruction of Jerusalem in 586 BCE). Ezra is given a magic potion, which enables him to write down, over the course of forty days and nights, not only the books of the Hebrew Bible but also seventy books of secret wisdom. Ezra is thus depicted as being instrumental in making available the books that are presently in the Hebrew canon. According to Grabbe, this narrative may reflect a genuine tradition, parallel to the one in the Hebrew Bible (where Ezra brings the Law from Babylon to Jerusalem) (Grabbe 1998: 90–1).

This portrayal of Ezra as the restorer of the Law brings Ezra on a par with and even superseding Moses. While Moses received the law, Ezra received the entire canon of the Hebrew Bible. In the case of Moses, God dictated and

Moses wrote; in the case of Ezra, Ezra dictated and his five scribes wrote (Feldman 1993: 192).

Even though the *Ezra Apocalypse* allegedly depicts events in the sixth century BCE, the text itself was written shortly after the Roman destruction of Jerusalem in 70 CE, probably during the reign of the Roman emperor, Domitian. Thus, the character of Ezra is a foil for the Jerusalem community in the first century CE, who had seen their city destroyed, and the Babylonians are a symbol of the Romans (Fried 2014: 4–5, 65–88). The *Ezra Apocalypse* was most likely composed in Hebrew, although we do not have any manuscripts which preserve this text. It was subsequently translated into a wide range of languages. In particular, the early Christian community translated it into Greek, yet we lack manuscripts which have preserved this early Greek translation. What we have instead are mediaeval copies of the Latin Vulgate, as well as Syriac, Ethiopic, Armenian and different Arabic translations of the Greek translation (Fried 2014: 65–6). At one point in the second century CE, Christian writers added two introductory chapters (called *5 Ezra*) to the beginning of the *Ezra Apocalypse* and two concluding chapters at the end (called *6 Ezra*) (Fried 2014: 4–5, 89–99).

Even later, mediaeval Christian writers were inspired by the visionary parts of *4 Ezra*, thus generating a wide range of Christian texts which employ the figure of Ezra in order to probe the nature of God's justice: the Greek *Apocalypse of Ezra*; the Latin *Vision of the Blessed Ezra*; the Armenian *Questions of Ezra*; and *The Apocalypse of Sedrach*. In their expansions to the *Ezra Apocalypse*, these newer works depict how Ezra tours hell and, as he sees the way the sinners are being tortured there, he intercedes on their behalf. God, however, is unforgiving. The sinners had ample of opportunity to repent while living and their present suffering is their just reward (Fried 2014: 4–5, 100–12). Another two texts, namely, *The Syriac Apocalypse of Ezra* and *The Ethiopic Apocalypse of Ezra*, have a more political aim. They predict the destruction of the Muslims and, in the case of the Syriac text, the Christian recapture of Jerusalem (Fried 2014: 112–17).

Ezra in Samaritan tradition

The Samaritans, now a very small community living primarily in modern-day Israel (near Nablus/Shechem and in Holon near Tel Aviv), consider themselves to be the descendants of the people who remained in the

Northern Kingdom of Israel after its destruction by the Neo-Assyrian armies in 721 BCE. In contrast, according to Jewish tradition, they are the descendants of those foreigners whom the Neo-Assyrians had settled in Israel while exiling the original population (2 Kings 17.5-6, 24; Ezra 4.1-2). The key point of contention between the two groups pertains to the correct place of worship: the Jews uphold that Jerusalem is God's chosen place; the Samaritans maintain that God has chosen Mt Gerizim as the sacred place.

There are significant differences between the MT of the Pentateuch and the Samaritan version of the same text. These discrepancies have given rise to the Samaritan tradition, stemming from the Middle Ages, that the Samaritans had the true Torah, while the Jews had falsified the biblical text. Ezra, being responsible for the writing down of the (Jewish) Torah, had thus remembered the Law incorrectly (Fried 2014: 126, citing the Islamic historian and geographer al-Mas'udi [896–956 CE]).

The tradition of a falsified Torah gained momentum in Islamic writings. Ibn Abi al-Hasan al-Samiri al-Danafi (Abu 'l-Fath) writing in 1355 CE, records a discussion between Sanballat, the governor of Samaria (e.g. Neh. 6.1-14) and Zerubbabel, the governor of Yehud, in the presence of the Persian monarch as to where the temple should be built. The Jewish text is thrown into the fire and goes up in flames; the Samaritan text is also thrown into the fire but leaps up in the air and comes out of the fire. The message of this narrative is that while the Jewish text stems from men, the Samaritan version stems from God. After this event, so Abu 'l-Fath, Ezra and Zerubbabel created a new alphabet, tampered with the Law, and cut out many passages (particularly those relating to Mt Gerizim) (Fried, 2014: 126–8, citing the chronicle of Abu 'l-Fath, 77).

Ezra in Islamic tradition

Ezra, called Uzair in Arabic, is according to Muslim tradition buried on the banks of the Tigris, near Basra in modern-day Iraq. The place, Al-'Uzair (named after Ezra), is a pilgrimage site for the local Muslims and Jews (Fried 2014: 136–7). Ezra/Uzair is known in Muslim traditions in three ways.

First, as in the above-mentioned Samaritan tradition, he is known as the falsifier of the Torah. Although not mentioned by name, the Qur'an (2.75; 3.78; 4.46; 5.13) accuses the Jews of having deliberately falsified the biblical text. More explicitly, Ibn Ḥazm states in his writings that Ezra is the one who wrote all the malicious lies about the patriarchs, as well as all the other disreputable and impious things that are written in the Hebrew Bible. In parallel, as the extant Torah: (1) does not reveal the coming of Mohammed; and (2) does not speak about the resurrection of the dead, a crucial tenet of faith in the Qur'an, it follows, so the argument goes, that the Jewish Torah cannot be the original one (Fried 2014: 4–5, 133–7).

Secondly, the Qur'an (2.259) refers to an anonymous person, who is often identified with Ezra/Uzair, who questions predestination and who doubts God's ability to raise the dead (Fried 2014: 132–3, citing Al Imam Ibn Kathir, *Stories of the Quran*).

Thirdly, the Qur'an (9.29-31) compares Ezra/Uzair with Jesus. According to this surah, Ezra is known as the 'son of God' whom the Jews worship, in contrast to Jesus who is known as the 'son of God' whom the Christians worship. The text wishes that Allah may destroy them both, as they are deluded about the truth (Fried 2014: 129–32; Feldman 1993: 193). Thus, although most Muslims are aware of the fact that the Jews deny worshipping Ezra, it nevertheless remains the case that God states this in the Qur'an.

Patristic writings on Ezra

Turning to patristic writing, there is a surprising lack of material relating to Ezra-Nehemiah in the writings of the Church Fathers. There are, however, a few exceptions. The so-called *Apocryphon of Jeremiah*, for example (a text which exists in several versions: Coptic, Arabic, Garshuni), contains a story about Ezra in its narrative about Jeremiah. This text, sometimes also referred to as *History of the Captivity in Babylon*, probably originated as a Jewish work, to which Christian elements were subsequently added. The earliest fragment stems from the seventh century CE, but the text itself is in all likelihood older. It tells how Jeremiah is taken to Babylon (rather than to Egypt as Jer. 43–44 claims) where he encounters the young schoolboy Ezra, a boy who is mocked by the Babylonians, prays to the God of Israel, and performs miracles (Kuhn 1991: 170–1; Fried 2014: 120–1).

Other Christian writers depict Ezra in a more negative light. Justin Martyr, in his *Dialogue with Trypho the Jew*, accuses the Jews of having removed those parts of the Hebrew Bible which predict the coming of Jesus (Fried 2014: 121). More explicitly, Porphyry of Tyre, in his *Adversus*

Christianos, states that Ezra falsified the Torah when he rewrote it after the exile. The presumed original text had been burnt together with the temple in 586 BCE. The presumed original Torah predicted the coming of Jesus more clearly (Fried 2014: 122).

Bede

The significant exception to the Christian neglect of Ezra-Nehemiah is the commentary by Bede (672/673–735 CE, a monk living in the north-east of England). The writings of Bede on Ezra and Nehemiah (*In Ezram et Neemiam*) is the only complete commentary of its time on these two books in the Hebrew Bible. It belongs firmly in the tradition of the Latin Fathers in its typological, tropological (moral), and allegorical exegesis. Because it is unique of its kind, we shall explore it in detail.

Bede considers Cyrus to be a type for Jesus. Just as Cyrus, after destroying the Babylonian Empire, freed the people of God and sent them back to their homeland and commanded them to build the temple, taking care that Jeremiah's words (Jer. 29.10-14) would be fulfilled, so Jesus destroyed the kingdom of the Devil and called back his elect and gathered them to his Church (Bede 1.1: 12-14). In a similar way, combining the statement in Ezra 3.10-13 with that in Hag. 2.9 that both compare the first and the second temple, Bede maintains that the first temple stands for the old covenant while the new temple stands for the new covenant. In the former, the Law and the Prophets were taught; in the new temple, Jesus and the apostles spread the Good News of the coming of the Kingdom of Heaven (Bede 1.4: 66). Further, the adversaries of Judah and Benjamin mentioned in Ezra 4.1-5 function as a symbol for 'false brothers', that is, heretics, as well as evil people within the Church (Bede 1.4: 67-68).

Bede further sees Ezra as yet another type for Jesus. Ezra, whose name means 'helper', brought the Jews from captivity in Babylon to freedom in Jerusalem. On a spiritual level, they were thus brought from 'confusion' (Babel) to 'peace' (Jerusalem) (Bede 2.9; 2.14: 112-13, 151). Artaxerxes and Darius symbolize Christian monarchs, who love and assist God's servants and who support the Christian Church (Bede 2.9: 117). The vessels that are brought from Babylon to Judah with the returning exiles (Ezra 8.25) represent the souls of those people who had converted to faith in God from the confusion and sins of this world. The twelve priests (Ezra 8.24) to whom

Ezra entrusts the vessels stand for the twelve apostles whose teaching enabled the Church to be established throughout the world (Bede 2.11; 129-30). The fact that Ezra and his followers waited and rested for three days upon arrival in Jerusalem after their journey represents the three virtues of faith, hope, and love. Bede explains that teachers need to be strong and prepared, sound in faith and action, before embarking upon their service. Teachers can educate their flocks only after being able to show these virtues themselves (Bede 2.11: 133).

As to the marriage crisis, Bede reinterprets it to be all about disassociating oneself from the detestable actions of the Gentiles. The foreign women represent figuratively followers of heresies and philosophers who, when admitted into the Church, contaminate the holy seed (Bede 2.12: 138-39). Just like women do, these heresies tempt, seduce and entice the faithful. Once this baseness is cast out, the beauty of chasteness will return (Bede 2.14: 150-51).

Turning to the book of Nehemiah, Bede continues in the same vein and locates types for Jesus and the Church. Like Ezra, Nehemiah too prefigures Jesus. Jesus' request to the Father to send 'another consoler' (*Paraclete*) in Jn 14.16 refers, according to Bede, to Nehemiah (the name meaning 'the Lord is my consoler'). Nehemiah did what Jesus did: he built up Jerusalem, he gathered the exiles of Israel, and he healed the broken-hearted (Bede 3.15: 154). Nehemiah is also a model for spiritual teachers. His habit of wandering around inspecting the various parts of the devastated city and of looking for ways in which it could be repaired can be compared with good spiritual leaders who get up regularly at night and inspect with scrutiny the state of the Church (Bede 3.17: 161). Finally, Nehemiah is yet again a type for Jesus in his zeal in the mixed marriage crisis. Bede compares his actions with those of Jesus when he scourged the temple (Mt. 21.12; Jn 2.14-15) (Bede 3.35: 222). Further, like Cyrus, Artaxerxes is a type for Jesus as he ended the captivity of the people of God and decreed that the temple could be restored (Bede 3.16: 158-59).

Bede furthermore finds typological meaning in the names of the city gates (Neh. 3.1-32). The 'fish gate' represents the flock of the Lord's faithful who are often called 'fish' (cf. Mt. 4.19; 13.48), the 'dung gate' represents those ordained to the Christian ministry who make sure that corrupt people are kept away from the Church (cf. Ps. 101.8), and the 'wall of the pool of Shelah' (Hebrew 'send') stands for those whom God has 'sent' to illuminate us. Finally, the 'horse gate' speaks of the Gentiles who have been converted to the Lord, while the priests who were repairing the 'horse gate' represent those missionaries who went on to spread the gospel to the nations (Bede 3.18: 164-65). Along the same lines of thinking, the different postings of the men on the wall (Neh. 4.10-14) and the division of labour (half of the people working, while the other half were fighting, Neh. 4.15-21) reveal that the Church contains many different types of people. Some build up the Church with good deeds, while others, armed with Scripture, keep vigilant for heretics who attack the same Church (Bede 3.20: 182-83). In a similar manner, Bede interprets the statement that while some people settled in Jerusalem, other people settled in the other cities in Judah as referring to the different stages and callings of a Christian's life: while some people are content to follow the Ten Commandments, others 'try to lay hold of the narrower stronghold of the perfect life' (Bede 3.13: 206).

In a few cases, Bede maintains the importance of the plain meaning of the text. In the case of Neh. 5, for example, which mentions that many of the poor people in Judah were starving and that others in society were mistreating them and adding to their suffering, Bede declares that in times of famine, we should give to the poor what we can and we should also forgive them any outstanding debt that they own us, so that God might forgive us our debts (Mt. 6.12) (Bede 3.21: 183-86).

Bibliography of key studies

Bede: On Ezra and Nehemiah. Translated with an Introduction and Notes by Scott DeGregorio (Translated Texts for Historians, 47; Liverpool: Liverpool University Press, 2006).

Feldman, Louis H. 'The Importance of Josephus for Reconstructing the Period of Restoration', in James M. Scott (ed.), *Restoration: Old Testament, Jewish, and Christian Perspective* (JSJS, 72; Leiden: Brill, 2001), pp. 223–61.

Fitzpatrick-McKinley, Anne. 'What did Nehemiah do for Judaism?' in Zuleika Rodgers, with Margaret Daly-Denton and Anne Fitzpatrick-McKinley (eds), *A Wandering Galilean: Essays in Honour of Seán Freyne* (SJSJ, 132; Leiden: Brill, 2008), pp. 93–117.

Fried, Lisbeth S. *Ezra and the Law in History and Tradition* (Studies on Personalities of the Old Testament; Columbia, SC: University of South Caroline Press, 2014).

Grabbe, Lester L. 'Josephus and the Reconstruction of the Judean Restoration', *JBL* 106 (1987), pp. 231–46.

Harrington, Hannah K. 'Intermarriage in Qumran Texts: The Legacy of Ezra-Nehemiah', in Christian Frevel (ed.), *Mixed Marriages: Intermarriage and Group Identity in the Second Temple Period* (LHBOTS, 547; London: T&T Clark, 2011), pp. 251–79.

Japhet, Sara. 'Sheshbazzar and Zerubbabel: Against the Background of the Historical and Religious Tendencies of Ezra-Nehemiah', *ZAW* 94 (1982), pp. 66–98.

Marttila, Marko. *Foreign Nations in the Wisdom of Ben Sira: A Jewish Sage between Opposition and Assimilation* (Deuterocanonical and Cognate Literature Studies, 13; Berlin/Boston: de Gruyter, 2012).

Porton, Gary G. 'Ezra in Rabbinic Literature', in James M. Scott (ed.), *Restoration: Old Testament, Jewish, and Christian Perspective* (JSJS, 72; Leiden: Brill, 2001), pp. 305–33.

Rabinowitz, Rabbi Yosef. *Nehemiah* (ArtScroll Tanach Series; Brooklyn, NY: Mesorah Publications, 1990).

Bibliography

Alt, Albrecht. *Die Rolle Samarias bei der Entstehung des Judentums* (Kleine Schriften zur Geschichte des Volkes Israel, Vol. 2 (Munich: Beck, 1953).

Angel, Hayyim. 'The Literary Significance of the Name Lists in Ezra-Nehemiah', *Jewish Bible Quarterly* 35 (2007), pp. 143–52.

Avigad, Nahum. *Bullae and Seals from a Post-Exilic Judaean Archive* (Qedem Monographs of the Institute of Archaeology, 4; Jerusalem: Hebrew University Press, 1976).

Becking, Bob. 'Continuity and Community: The Belief System of the Book of Ezra', in B. Becking and M. C. A. Korpel (eds), *The Crisis of Israelite Religion: Transformation of Religious Tradition in Exilic and Post-Exilic Times* (OtS, 42; Leiden: Brill, 1999), pp. 256–75. Reprinted in Becking, Bob. *Ezra, Nehemiah, and the Construction of Jewish Identity* (FAT, 80: Tübingen: Mohr Siebeck, 2011), pp. 24–42.

Becking, Bob. 'The Story of the Three Youth and the Composition of 1 Esdras', in Lisbeth S. Fried (ed.), *Was 1 Esdras First? An Investigation into the Priority and Nature of 1 Esdras* (Ancient Israel and Its Literature, 7; Atlanta, GA: SBL, 2011), pp. 61–71.

Bede: On Ezra and Nehemiah. Translated with an Introduction and Notes by Scott DeGregorio (Translated Texts for Historians, 47; Liverpool: Liverpool University Press, 2006).

Bedford, Peter R. 'Temple Funding and Priestly Authority in Achaemenid Judah', in Jonathan Stökl and Caroline Waerzeggers (eds), *Exile and Return: The Babylonian Context* (BZAW, 478; Berlin: de Gruyter, 2015), pp. 336–51.

Blenkinsopp, Joseph. *Ezra-Nehemiah* (OTL; Philadelphia, PA: Westminster Press, 1988).

Blenkinsopp, Joseph. 'Was the Pentateuch the Civic and Religious Constitution of the Jewish Ethnos in the Persian Period?' in James W. Watts (ed.), *Persia and Torah: The Theory of Imperial Authorization of the Pentateuch* (SBL Symposium Series, 17: Atlanta, GA: SBL, 2001), pp. 41–62.

Boda, Mark J. 'Confession as Theological Expression: Ideological Origins of Penitential Prayers', in Mark J. Boda, Daniel K. Falk and Rodney A. Werline (eds), *Seeking the Favour of God: The Origins of Penitential Prayer in Second Temple Judaism*, Vol. 1 (Early Judaism and its Literature, 21; Atlanta, GA: SBL, 2006), pp. 21–50.

Boda, Mark J. *Praying the Tradition: The Origin and Use of Tradition in Nehemiah 9* (BZAW, 277; Berlin: de Gruyter, 1999).

Briant, Pierre. *From Cyrus to Alexander: A History of the Persian Empire* (trans. Peter T. Daniels; Winona Lake, IN: Eisenbraun, 2002).

Burt, Sean. *The Courtier and the Governor: Transformations of Genre in the Nehemiah Memoir* (JAJS, 17; Göttingen: Vandenhoeck & Ruprecht, 2014).

Cataldo, Jeremiah W. *A Theocratic Yehud? Issues of Government in a Persian Province* (LHBOTS, 498; T&T Clark: New York, 2009).

Childs, Brevard S. *Introduction to the Old Testament as Scripture* (Philadelphia, PA: Fortress, 1979).

Ciampa, Roy E. and Brian S. Rosner. 'Corinthians', in G. K. Beale and D. A. Carson (eds), *Commentary of the New Testament Use of the Old Testament* (Nottingham: Apollos, 2007), pp. 695–752.

Cornell, Stephen. 'That's the Story of Our Life', in Paul R. Spickard and W. Jeffrey Burroughs (eds), *We Are a People: Narrative and Multiplicity in Constructing Ethnic Identity* (Asian American History and Culture; Philadelphia: Temple University Press, 2000), pp. 41–53.

COS = *The Context of Scripture* (eds William W. Hallo and K. Lawson Younger, Jr.); Vol. 2: *Monumental Inscriptions* (Leiden: Brill, 2000); Vol. 3: *Archival Documents from the Hebrew Bible* (Leiden: Brill, 2003).

Dandamayev, Muhammad. 'Achaemenid Imperial Policies and Provincial Governments', *Iranica Antiqua* 34 (1999), pp. 269–82.

Douglas, Mary. 'Responding to Ezra: The Priests and the Foreign Wives', *Biblical Interpretation* 10 (2002), pp. 1–23.

Duggan, Michael W. *The Covenant Renewal in Ezra-Nehemiah, (Neh 7:72b-10:40): An Exegetical, Literary, and Theological Study* (SBLDS, 164; Atlanta, GA: SBL, 2001).

Eskenazi, Tamara Cohn. *In an Age of Prose: A Literary Approach to Ezra-Nehemiah* (SBLMS, 36: Atlanta, GA: Scholars Press, 1988).

Eskenazi, Tamara Cohn. 'Out of the Shadows: Biblical Women in the Postexilic Era', *JSOT* 54 (1992), pp. 25–43.

Eskenazi, Tamara Cohn. 'Nehemiah 9–10: Structure and Significance', *JHS* 2001, sections 2.1., 2.2., and 4.3. http://www.jhsonline.org/cocoon/JHS/a021.html.

Esler, Philip F. 'Ezra-Nehemiah as a Narrative of (Re-Invented) Israelite Identity', *Biblical Interpretation* 11, no. 3 (2003), pp. 413–26.

Faust, Avraham. *Judah in the Neo-Babylonian Period: The Archaeology of Desolation* (Archaeology and Biblical Studies, 18; Atlanta, GA: SBL, 2012).

Feldman, Louis H. 'The Importance of Josephus for Reconstructing the Period of Restoration', in James M. Scott (ed.), *Restoration: Old Testament, Jewish, and Christian Perspective* (JSJS, 72; Leiden: Brill, 2001), pp. 223–61.

Feldman, Louis H. 'Josephus' Portrait of Ezra', *VT* 43 (1993), pp. 190–214.

Fensham, Charles. *The Books of Ezra and Nehemiah* (NICOT; Grand Rapids, MI: Eerdmans, 1982).

Fitzpatrick-McKinley, Anne. 'What did Nehemiah do for Judaism?' in Zuleika Rodgers, with Margaret Daly-Denton and Anne Fitzpatrick-McKinley (eds), *A Wandering Galilean: Essays in Honour of Seán Freyne* (SJSJ, 132; Leiden: Brill, 2008), pp. 93–117.

Frei, Peter. 'Persian Imperial Authorization: A Summary', in James W. Watts (ed.), *Persia and Torah: The Theory of Imperial Authorization of the Pentateuch* (SBL Symposium Series, 17: Atlanta, GA: SBL, 2001), pp. 5–40.

Fried, Lisbeth S. *Ezra: A Commentary* (Critical Commentaries; Sheffield: Phoenix, 2015).

Fried, Lisbeth S. *Ezra and the Law in History and Tradition* (Studies on Personalities of the Old Testament; Columbia, SC: University of South Caroline Press, 2014).

Fried, Lisbeth S. *The Priest and the Great King: Temple-Palace Relations in the Persian Empire* (Biblical and Judaic Studies from the University of California, San Diego, 10; Winona Lake, IN: Eisenbrauns, 2004).

Fried, Lisbeth S. 'Temple Building in Ezra 1–6', in Mark J. Boda and Jamie Novotny (eds), *From the Foundations to the Crenellations: Essays on Temple building in the Ancient Near East* and *Hebrew Bible* (AOAT, 366; Münster: Ugarit-Verlag, 2010), pp. 319–55.

Fried, Lisbeth S. '"You Shall Appoint Judges": Ezra's Mission and the Rescript of Artaxerxes', in James W. Watts (ed.), *Persia and Torah: The Theory of Imperial Authorization of the Pentateuch* (SBL Symposium Series, 17: Atlanta, GA: SBL, 2001), pp. 63–89.

Fried, Lisbeth S. (ed.), *Was 1 Esdras First? An Investigation into the Priority and Nature of 1 Esdras* (Ancient Israel and Its Literature, 7; Atlanta, GA: SBL, 2011).

Fulton, Deirdre N. *Reconsidering Nehemiah's Judah* (FAT, II/80; Tübingen: Mohr Siebeck, 2015).

Fulton, Deirdre N. and Gary Knoppers, 'Lower Criticism and Higher Criticism: The Case of 1 Esdras', in Lisbeth S. Fried (ed.), *Was 1 Esdras First? An Investigation into the Priority and Nature of 1 Esdras* (Ancient Israel and Its Literature, 7; Atlanta, GA: SBL, 2011), pp. 11–31 (17, 24–5).

Grabbe, Lester L. *Ezra-Nehemiah* (Old Testament Readings; London and New York: Routledge, 1998).

Grabbe, Lester L. 'Josephus and the Reconstruction of the Judean Restoration', *JBL* 106 (1987), pp. 231–46.

Grabbe, Lester L. 'The Law of Moses in the Ezra Tradition: More Virtual Than Real?' in James W. Watts (ed.), *Persia and Torah: The Theory of Imperial Authorization of the Pentateuch* (SBL Symposium Series, 17: Atlanta, GA: SBL, 2001), pp. 91–113.

Grabbe, Lester L. 'The "Persian Documents" in the Book of Ezra: Are They Authentic?' in Oded Lipschits and Manfred Oeming (eds), *Judah and the Judeans in the Persian Period* (Winona Lake, IN: Eisenbrauns, 2006), pp. 531–70.

Grätz, Sebastian. *Das Edikt des Artaxerxes: Eine Untersuchung zum religionspolitischen und historischen Umfeld von Esra 7,12-26* (BZAW, 337; Berlin; de Gruyter, 2004).

Harrington, Hannah K. 'Holiness and Purity in Ezra-Nehemiah', in Mark J. Boda and Paul L. Redditt (eds), *Unity and Disunity in Ezra-Nehemiah: Redactor, Rhetoric, and Reader* (HBM, 17; Sheffield: Sheffield Phoenix Press, 2008), pp. 98–116.

Harrington, Hannah K. 'Intermarriage in Qumran Texts: The Legacy of Ezra-Nehemiah', in Christian Frevel (ed.), *Mixed Marriages: Intermarriage and Group Identity in the Second Temple Period* (LHBOTS, 547; London: T&T Clark, 2011), pp. 251–79.

Hayes, Christine. 'Intermarriage and Impurity in Ancient Jewish Sources', *HTR* 92 (1999), pp. 3–36.

Heger, Paul. *Women in the Bible, Qumran,* and *Early Rabbinic Literature: Their Status* and *Roles* (STDJ, 110; Leiden: Brill, 2014).

Hoglund, Kenneth G. *Achaemenid Imperial Administration in Syria-Palestine and the Missions of Ezra and Nehemiah* (SBLDS, 125; Atlanta, GA: Scholars Press, 1992).

Hutchinson, John and Anthony Smith. 'Introduction', in John Hutchinson and Anthony Smith (eds), *Ethnicity* (Oxford Readers; Oxford: Oxford University Press, 1996), pp. 3–14.

Janzen, David. 'The Crisis in Jerusalem: Ethnic, Cultic, Legal and Geographic Boundaries in Ezra-Nehemiah', in Mark J. Boda and Paul L. Redditt (eds), *Unity and Disunity in Ezra-Nehemiah: Redactor, Rhetoric, and Reader* (HBM, 17; Sheffield: Sheffield Phoenix Press, 2008), pp. 117–35.

Janzen, David. *Witch-hunts, Purity and Social Boundaries: The Expulsion of the Foreign Women in Ezra 9–10* (JSOTS, 350; Sheffield: Sheffield Academic Press, 2002).

Japhet, Sara. 'Composition and Chronology in the Book of Ezra-Nehemiah', in Tamara C. Eskenazi and Kent H. Richards (eds), *Second Temple Studies: Vol. 2. Temple and Community in the Persian Period* (JSOTS, 175; Sheffield: JSOT Press, 1994), pp. 189–216. Reprinted in Sara Japhet, *From the rives of Babylon to the Highlands of Judah: Collected Studies on the Restoration Period* (Winona Lake, IN: Eisenbrauns, 2011), pp. 245–67.

Japhet, Sara. '1 Esdras: Its Genre, Literary Form, and Goals', in Lisbeth S. Fried (ed.), *Was 1 Esdras First? An Investigation into the Priority and Nature of 1 Esdras* (Ancient Israel and Its Literature 7; Atlanta, GA: SBL, 2011), pp. 209–24.

Japhet, Sara. 'The Expulsion of the Foreign Women (Ezra 9–10): The Legal
    Basis, Precedents, and Consequences for the Definition of Jewish Identity',
    in Friedhelm Hartenstein and Michael Pietsch (eds), '*Sieben Augen auf
    einem Stein*' (*Sach 3,9*): *Studien zur Literatur des Zweiten Temples. Festschrift
    für Ina Willi-Plein zum 65. Geburtstag* (Neukirchen-Vluyn: Neukirchener
    Verlag, 2007), pp. 141–61.
Japhet, Sara. 'Sheshbazzar and Zerubbabel: Against the Background of the
    Historical and Religious Tendencies of Ezra-Nehemiah', *ZAW* 94 (1982),
    pp. 66–98.
Japhet, Sara. 'The Supposed Common Authorship of Chronicles and Ezra-
    Nehemiah Investigated Anew', *VT* 18 (1968), pp. 330–71.
Jigoulov, Vadim. 'Administration of Achaemenid Phoenicia: A Case for
    Managed Autonomy', in Gary N. Knoppers and Lester L. Grabbe with
    Deirdre Fulton (eds), *Exile and Restoration Revisited: Essays on the
    Babylonian and Persian Periods in Memory of Peter R. Ackroyd* (LSTS, 73;
    London: T&T Clark, 2009), pp. 138–51.
Johnson, Willa M. *The Holy Seed Has Been Defiled: The Interethnic Marriage
    Dilemma in Ezra 9–10* (HBM, 33; Sheffield: Sheffield Phoenix Press, 2011).
Karrer, Christiane. *Ringen um die Verfassung Judas: Eine Studie zu den
    theologisch-politischen Vorstellungen im Esra-Nehemia-Buch* (BZAW, 308;
    Berlin: de Gruyter, 2001).
Kessler, John. 'Persia's Loyal Yahwists: Power Identity and Ethnicity in
    Achaemenid Yehud', in Oded Lipschits and Manfred Oeming (eds), *Judah
    and the Judeans in the Persian Period* (Winona Lake, IN: Eisenbrauns, 2006),
    pp. 91–121.
Klawans, Jonathan. 'Idolatry, Incest, and Impurity: Moral Defilement in
    Ancient Judaism', *JSJ* 29, no. 4 (1998), pp. 391–415.
Knoppers, Gary N. 'An Achaemenid Imperial Authorization of Torah in
    Yehud?' in James W. Watts (ed.), *Persia and Torah: The Theory of Imperial
    Authorization of the Pentateuch* (SBL Symposium Series, 17: Atlanta, GA:
    SBL, 2001), pp. 115–34.
Kraemer, David. 'On the Relationship of the Books of Ezra and Nehemiah',
    JSOT 59 (1993), pp. 73–92.
Kuhn, K. H. 'Apocryphon of Jeremia', in Aziz S. Atiya (ed.), *The Coptic
    Encyclopedia* (New York, NY: Macmillan, 1991), 1:170–1.
Leuchter, Mark. 'The Book of the Twelve and "The Great Assembly"', in Rainer
    Albertz, James D. Nogalski and Jakob Wöhrle (eds), *Perspectives on the
    Formation of the Book of the Twelve: Methodological Foundations,
    Redactional Processes, Historical Insights* (BZAW, 433: Berlin: de Gruyter,
    2012), pp. 337–52.
Lipschits, Oded. 'Achaemenid Imperial Policy, Settlement Processes in
    Palestine, and the Status of Jerusalem in the Middle of the Fifth Century

B.C.E.', in Oded Lipschits and Manfred Oeming (eds), *Judah and the Judeans in the Persian Period* (Winona Lake, IN: Eisenbrauns, 2006), pp. 19–52.

Lipschits, Oded and Manfred Oeming (eds), *Judah and the Judeans in the Persian Period* (Winona Lake, IN: Eisenbrauns, 2006).

Marttila, Marko. *Foreign Nations in the Wisdom of Ben Sira: A Jewish Sage between Opposition and Assimilation* (Deuterocanonical and Cognate Literature Studies, 13; Berlin/Boston: de Gruyter, 2012).

Milgrom, Jacob. *Cult and Conscience: The Asham and the Priestly Doctrine of Repentance* (SJLA, 18; Leiden: Brill, 1976).

Min, Kyung-jin. *The Levitical Authorship of Ezra-Nehemiah* (JSOTS, 409; London: T & T Clark International, 2004).

Moffat, Donald P. *Ezra's Social Drama: Identity Formation, Marriage and Social Conflict in Ezra 9 and 10* (LHBOTS, 579; London: T&T Clark, 2013).

Newman, Judith H. *Praying by the Book: The Scripturalization of Prayer in Second Temple Judaism* (Early Judaism and its Literature, 14; Atlanta, GA: Scholars Press, 1999).

Olyan, Saul M. 'Purity Ideology in Ezra-Nehemiah as a Tool to Reconstitute the Community', *JSJ* 35, no. 1 (2004), pp. 1–16.

Pakkala, Juha. *Ezra the Scribe: The Development of Ezra 7–10 and Nehemiah 8* (BZAW, 347; Berlin; de Gruyter, 2004).

Pakkala, Juha. 'Why 1 Esdras Is Probably Not an Early Version of the Ezra-Nehemiah Tradition', in Lisbeth S. Fried (ed.), *Was 1 Esdras First? An Investigation into the Priority and Nature of 1 Esdras* (Ancient Israel and Its Literature, 7; Atlanta, GA: SBL, 2011), pp. 93–107.

Porton, Gary G. 'Ezra in Rabbinic Literature', in James M. Scott (ed.), *Restoration: Old Testament, Jewish, and Christian Perspective* (JSJS, 72; Leiden: Brill, 2001), pp. 305–33.

Rabinowitz, Rabbi Yosef. *Nehemiah* (ArtScroll Tanach Series; Brooklyn, NY: Mesorah Publications, 1990).

Redditt, Paul L. 'The Dependence of Ezra-Nehemiah on 1 and 2 Chronicles', in Mark H. Boda and Paul L. Redditt (eds), *Unity and Disunity in Ezra-Nehemiah: Redaction, Rhetoric, and Reader* (HBM, 17; Sheffield: Sheffield Phoenix Press, 2008), pp. 216–40.

Reinmuth, Titus. *Der Bericht Nehemiahs: Zur literarischen Eigenart traditionsgeschichtlichen Prägung und innerbiblischen Rezeption des ich-Berichts Nehemias* (OBO, 183; Göttingen: Vandenhoeck & Ruprecht, 2002).

Reinmuth, Titus. 'Nehemiah 8 and the Authority of Torah in Ezra-Nehemiah', in Mark J. Boda and Paul L. Redditt (eds), *Unity and Disunity in Ezra-Nehemiah: Redactor, Rhetoric, and Reader* (HBM, 17; Sheffield: Sheffield Phoenix Press, 2008), pp. 241–62.

Rom-Shiloni, Dalit. *Exclusive Inclusivity: Identity Conflicts between the Exiles and the People who Remained (6th–5th Centuries BCE)* (LHBOTS, 543; London: T&T Clark, 2013).

Rothenbusch, Ralf. '*… Abgesondert zur Tora Gottes hin*': *Ethnische und religiöse Identitäten im Ezra/Nehemiabuch* (Herders biblische Studien, 70; Freiburg: Herder, 2012).

Schaper, Joachim. 'The Jerusalem Temple as an Instrument of the Achaemenid Fiscal Administration', *VT* 45 (1995), pp. 528–39.

Schenker, Adrian. 'The Relationship between Ezra-Nehemiah and 1 Esdras', in Lisbeth S. Fried (ed.), *Was 1 Esdras First? An Investigation into the Priority and Nature of 1 Esdras* (Ancient Israel and Its Literature, 7; Atlanta, GA: SBL, 2011), pp. 45–60.

Schottroff, Willy. '*Gedenken*' *im alten Orient und im Alten Testament: Die Wurzel Zākar im semitischen Sprachkreis* (WMANT, 15; Neukirchen-Vluyn: Neukirchener, 1964).

Ska, Jean Louis. '"Persian Imperial Authorization": Some Question Marks', in James W. Watts (ed.), *Persia and Torah: The Theory of Imperial Authorization of the Pentateuch* (SBL Symposium Series, 17: Atlanta, GA: SBL, 2001), pp. 161–82.

Slotan-Sivan, H. 'The Silent Woman of Yehud: Notes on Ezra 9–10', *JJS* 51 (2000), pp. 3–18.

Smith-Christopher, David L. 'The Mixed Marriage Crisis in Ezra 9–10 and Nehemiah 13: A Study of the Sociology of the Post-exilic Judean Community', in Tamara C. Eskenazi and Kent H. Richards (eds), *Second Temple Studies 2: Temple and Community in the Persian Period* (JSOTS, 175; Sheffield, England: JSOT Press, 1994), pp. 243–65.

Southwood, Katherine E. *Ethnicity and the Mixed Marriage Crisis in Ezra 9–10: An Anthropological Approach* (OTM; Oxford: Oxford University Press, 2012).

Spark, Kenton L. *Ethnicity and Identity in Ancient Israel: Prolegomena to the Study of Ethnic Sentiments and their Expression in the Hebrew Bible* (Winona Lake, IN: Eisenbrauns, 1998).

Talmon, Shemaryahu. 'Ezra and Nehemiah', in Robert Alter and Frank Kermode (eds), *The Literary Guide to the Bible* (Cambridge, MA: Harvard University Press, 1987), pp. 357–64.

Talshir, Zipora. 'Ancient Composition Patterns Mirrored in 1 Esdras and the Priority of the Canonical Composition Type', in Lisbeth S. Fried (ed.), *Was 1 Esdras First? An Investigation into the Priority and Nature of 1 Esdras* (Ancient Israel and Its Literature, 7; Atlanta, GA: SBL, 2011), pp. 109–30.

Tiemeyer, Lena-Sofia. 'Abraham, a Judahite Prerogative', *ZAW* 120 (2008), pp. 49–66.

Tiemeyer, Lena-Sofia. 'Hope and Disappointment: The Judahite Critique of the Exilic Leadership in Isaiah 56-66', in Rannfrid Thelle, Terje Stordalen,

Mervyn Richardson and Robert P. Gordon (eds), *New Perspectives on Old Testament Prophecy and History. FS Hans M. Barstad* (VTS, 168; Leiden: Brill, 2015), pp. 57–73.

Tiemeyer, Lena-Sofia. 'Sanballat', in Bill T. Arnold and H. G. M. Williamson (eds), *Dictionary of the Old Testament: Historical Books* (Leicester, England: Intervarsity Press, 2005), pp. 877–80.

Throntveit, Mark A. 'Linguistic Analysis and the Question of Authorship in Chronicles, Ezra and Nehemiah', *VT* 32 (1982), pp. 201–16.

Trevor-Roper, Hugh. 'The Invention of Tradition: The Highland Tradition of Scotland', in Eric J. Hobsbawm and Terence O. Ranger (eds), *The Invention of Tradition* (Cambridge: Cambridge University Press, 1983), pp. 15–41.

VanderKam, James C. 'Ezra-Nehemiah or Ezra and Nehemiah?' in Eugene Ulrich, John W. Wright, Robert P. Carroll and Philip R. Davies (eds), *Priests, Prophets and Scribes: Essays on the Formation and Heritage of Second Temple Judaism in Honour of Joseph Blenkinsopp* (JSOTS, 149: Sheffield, JSOT Press, 1992), pp. 55–75.

VanderKam, James C. 'Literary Questions between Ezra, Nehemiah, and 1 Esdras', in Lisbeth S. Fried (ed.), *Was 1 Esdras First? An Investigation into the Priority and Nature of 1 Esdras* (Ancient Israel and Its Literature, 7; Atlanta, GA: SBL, 2011), pp. 131–44.

Washington, H. C. 'The Strange Women of Proverbs 1–9 and Post-Exilic Society', in Tamara C. Eskenazi and Kent H. Richards (eds), *Second Temple Studies 2: Temple and Community in the Persian Period* (JSOTS, 175; Sheffield, England: JSOT Press, 1994), pp. 217–42.

Watts, James W. (ed.), *Persia and Torah: The Theory of Imperial Authorization of the Pentateuch* (SBL Symposium Series, 17: Atlanta, GA: SBL, 2001).

Weeks, Stuart D. E. 'Biblical Literature and the Emergence of Ancient Jewish Nationalism', *Biblical Interpretation* 10 (2002), pp. 144–57.

Weinberg, Joel. *The Citizen-Temple Community* (trans. Daniel L. Smith-Christopher (JSOTS, 151; Sheffield: Sheffield Academic Press, 1992).

Williamson, H. G. M. '1 Esdras as Rewritten Bible?' in Lisbeth S. Fried (ed.), *Was 1 Esdras First? An Investigation into the Priority and Nature of 1 Esdras* (Ancient Israel and Its Literature, 7; Atlanta, GA: SBL, 2011), pp. 237–50.

Williamson, H. G. M. 'The Composition of Ezra i–vi', *JTS* 34 (1983), pp. 1–30.

Williamson, H. G. M. *Ezra, Nehemiah* (WBC, 16; Waco, TX: Word Books, 1985).

Williamson, H. G. M. 'The Governors of Judah under the Persians', *Tyndale Bulletin* 39 (1988), pp. 59–82. Reprinted in his *Studies in Persian Period History* and *Historiography* (FAT, 38; Tübingen: Mohr Siebeck, 2004), pp. 46–62.

Williamson, H. G. M. *Israel in the Books of Chronicles* (Cambridge: Cambridge University Press, 1977).

Williamson, H. G. M. 'Review of J. Pakkala, *The Development of Ezra 7–10 and Nehemiah 8*', *JTS* 58 (2007), pp. 584–9.

Williamson, H. G. M. 'Review of Joel Weinberg, *The Citizen-Temple Community*', *VT* 45 (1995), p. 574.

Williamson H. G. M. 'Structure and Historiography in Nehemiah 9', in *Proceedings of the Ninth World Congress of Jewish Studies* (ed. Goshen-Gottstein; Jerusalem: Magnes, 1988), pp. 117–31. Reprinted in Williamson, H. G. M. *Studies in Persian Period History* and *Historiography* (FAT, 38; Tübingen: Mohr Siebeck, 2004), pp. 282–93.

Wright, Jacob L. *Rebuilding Identity: The Nehemiah-memoir and its Earliest Readers* (BZAW, 372; Berlin; de Gruyter, 2004).

Zeitlin, Solomon. 'Takkanot "Ezra"', *JQR* 8 (1917), pp. 61–74.

Index of Authors

Index of References